GARY COZZENS

TRES RITOS

A History of Three Rivers, New Mexico

I0805778

THE
History
PRESS

Published by The History Press
Charleston, SC 29403
www.historypress.net

Copyright © 2015 by Gary Cozzens
All rights reserved

First published 2015

Manufactured in the United States

ISBN 978.1.60949.883.2

Library of Congress Control Number: 2014956421

Notice: The information in this book is true and complete to the best of our knowledge. It is offered without guarantee on the part of the author or The History Press. The author and The History Press disclaim all liability in connection with the use of this book.

All rights reserved. No part of this book may be reproduced or transmitted in any form whatsoever without prior written permission from the publisher except in the case of brief quotations embodied in critical articles and reviews.

This book is respectfully dedicated to my uncles Wayne Cozzens, Doyle Cozzens and H.R. "Bob" Parsons Jr.

Contents

Acknowledgements

This is my third book to be published by The History Press. As with the previous two books on the Nogal Mesa and Capitan, many people assisted in the process.

Many sources record the history of Three Rivers; I have relied heavily on several. Janie Bell Furman wrote the quality book *In the Mountain's Shadow: Three Rivers Ranch* for the Tularosa Basin Historical Society. Other primary sources consulted include Charles L. Sonnichsen's *Tularosa* and William A. Keleher's *The Fabulous Frontier*. Joe Ben Sanders has written several books on the Three Rivers Petroglyph Site.

My good fortune has led me to Roberta Key Haldane, noted historian of Lincoln County and respected author. She made the first edit of this manuscript, and for that I am especially grateful. In addition to providing materials and leads to sources, she is a personal mentor and confidant.

G.L. Tucker of Tularosa, who grew up on the Hatchet Ranch, was a prime source of information and materials. He provided many resources and ideas, and to him I am thankful. Steven Spencer provided remembrances of the Hatchet Ranch. Barbara Jeanne Branum-Reily, a descendant of early settlers in Lincoln County, also provided invaluable support.

Special thanks to Kathleen Chamberlain and Fred Nolan for providing information on Susan McSween Barber and Billy the Kid at Three Rivers and to Bob Boze Bell for the use of his drawing of Billy the Kid. Also thanks to Janie Bell Furman, Cliff Caldwell and Paul O'Brien for material on Patrick Coghlan.

Thanks to Mark Santiago, director of the New Mexico Farm and Ranch Museum, for his review of early European activities in the Three Rivers area. Margaret Berrier, a noted petroglyph expert in southern New Mexico, reviewed the chapter on the Jornada Mogollon and the Three Rivers Petroglyph Site and provided some beautiful photographs of the petroglyphs. Cameron and Pamela Blagg, current owners of the Three Rivers Trading Post, provided information and photographs.

Thanks to my grandfather S.M. "Primo" Cozzens, who managed the Three Rivers farm for Thomas F. Ryan III in the late 1950s and early 1960s. His daughter Marilyn provided remembrances of growing up on the ranch, as did Mr. Ryan's daughter Victoria, who also provided photographs.

The Tularosa Basin Historical Society allowed me to use period photographs from its collection. The Rio Grande Historical Collections at New Mexico State University is a magnificent resource. I appreciate the help Teddy Payne Riehl and Elizabeth Villa provided during a visit there.

Pat Garrett and Raynene Greer at the Capitan Public Library were able to obtain books through interlibrary loan.

My first editor on this project, Jerry Roberts, was steadfast in his support despite my missing multiple deadlines. (This book was supposed to have been completed in the summer of 2013 but was delayed due to a major forest fire, the passing of my father and a new job.) Jerry patiently worked with me and adjusted deadline after deadline. For that I am grateful. Artie Crisp, who saw this book to completion, followed Jerry.

Richard Bryant helped with photographs once again. Pete Eidenbach provided critical comments. Mary Serna and Lynda Sanchez provided help and photographs dealing with the Mescalero Apaches.

Thanks to Rudy Acosta, a raft of sanity in a sea of insanity in my other world. My greatest appreciation goes to my wife, Shirley Crawford, for all she does…and, for Sam.

Introduction

At 12,003 feet above sea level, Sierra Blanca (White Mountain) dominates all of south central New Mexico. At the foot of Sierra Blanca lies the Three Rivers Valley through which the three streams that give it its name run: Three Rivers Creek, Indian Creek and Golondrina (Spanish for the broom snake plant) Creek. The rivers flow for thirty-three miles in a generally southwest direction into the Tularosa Basin.

Located on the eastern edge of the Tularosa Basin, Three Rivers Valley is Paleozoic rock that arched between the San Andres and Sacramento Mountains. The crust pulled apart, and the arch collapsed, leaving evidence of the linkage between the two mountains.

Southwest of Three Rivers are the White Sands, and almost directly due west is the lava flow known as the Malpais. The lava field's source, Little Black Peak on the bed's north end, is estimated to be about ten thousand years old. Farther across the basin to the west are the San Andres and Oscura Mountains. Northwest is the Chupadera Mesa, and the Godfrey Hills lie directly north.

Know originally as "Tres Ritos," this area has seen much history of New Mexico, from the habitation of the prehistoric people who left over twenty thousand petroglyphs, to the late 1880s of Susan McSween Barber and Billy the Kid. It was the homeland of the Mescalero Apache Tribe, as well as being involved in the Teapot Dome Scandal of the 1920s, which resulted in the first removal of a cabinet secretary.

Three Rivers is literally an oasis in the desert. In 1977, Human Systems Research, Inc., measured the flow of water from Indian Creek at a daily rate of 4,660 acre-feet, or 1.8 million gallons.[1] The flow of the creeks is irregular at best, and even today the water frequently goes underground. Even so, this type of water is rare in the desert Southwest and would thus be a perfect place to farm and ranch no matter the era.

DRAMATIS PERSONNEL

Three Rivers has a cast of characters to rival that of any other area of the same geographical size. To start with, two players were already well known for their roles in the Lincoln County War—William H. Bonney, also called Billy the Kid, and Susan McSween Barber. Joining them was Shanta Boy of the Mescalero Apaches, a man the equivalent of a millionaire in his world of surrounding villages. Shanta Boy's granddaughter Virginia Klinecole became the first president of the Mescalero Apache Tribe and was followed several years later by Sarah Misquez. Other players owning adjoining land were Thomas Fortune Ryan III, a bona fide pioneer in twentieth-century aviation, and Colin McMillan, a candidate for state lieutenant governor and national assistant secretary of defense.

Yet all of these prominent players are overshadowed by one stereotypical frontier New Mexican—Albert Bacon Fall. Fall was a defense attorney in two of the major trials of that period, trials he won seemingly with ease. He was also a district attorney, a representative to the territorial legislature, one of the first two United States senators to represent New Mexico after statehood in 1912 and the United States secretary of the interior.

Despite these accomplishments, as the result of the infamous Teapot Dome Scandal, Fall is best remembered as the first federal cabinet secretary in the United States to be convicted of bribery. In a highly charged political trial, Fall was found guilty of accepting a bribe (while, incredibly, the man accused of providing the bribe was found to be innocent). Hero or villain, Fall *is* Three Rivers.[2]

A NOTE ABOUT THE PHOTOGRAPHS

There are many period photographs of Three Rivers that are not included in this book. A significant number are of the Fall Ranch and family. Unfortunately, these photos are not in the public domain and, therefore, are not included in this book.

IF YOU VISIT

The Three Rivers of today is easily accessible. However, as in the days of Albert Bacon Fall, ranching remains a viable occupation, with property rights taken seriously. Additionally, the Three Rivers Mescalero Community is part of a sovereign nation. If you decide to visit either site, make sure you obtain permission to go on this land before you arrive.

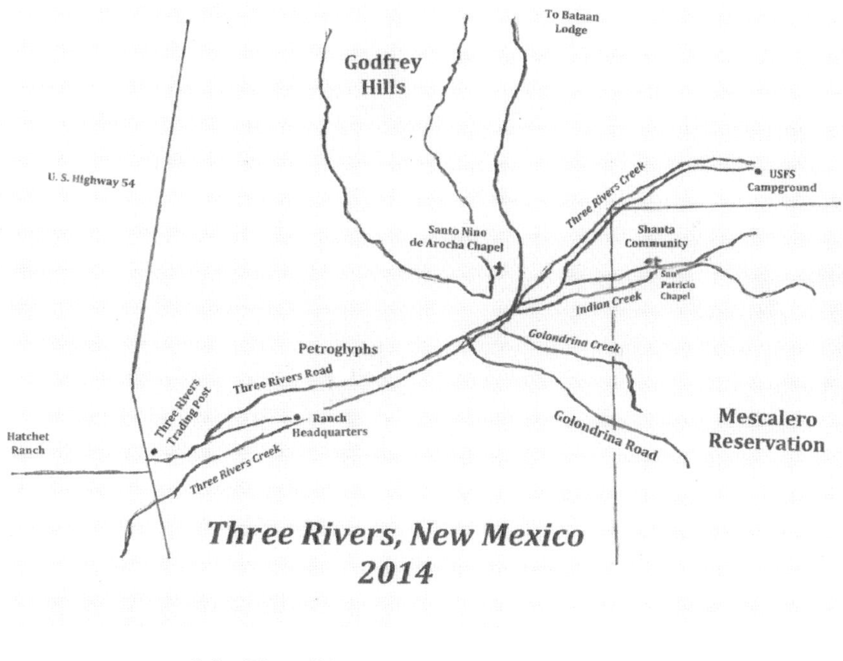

Contemporary map of the Three Rivers area. *Map by author.*

As you will read in the following pages, the whole valley is an archaeological site, and there are many artifacts scattered about. Please enjoy them where they lie and do not take them home with you. Additionally, should you visit the petroglyphs, please do not touch them, as the oil in your fingers destroys the patina.

1

The Jornada Mogollon

The earliest inhabitants of the region were the Paleo-Indians. Traces of these people have been found at Mockingbird Gap at the northern end of the Tularosa Basin above Chupadera Mesa at an intermittently occupied campsite.

About AD 200, the first major inhabitants of Three Rivers migrated into the area. While we do not know the name these people called themselves, they are now known as the Jornada Mogollon. *Jornada* means "journey" in Spanish; Mogollon comes from Juan Flores Mogollon, governor of New Mexico in 1715. These people occupied the region from about AD 200 to 1450, when the area was abandoned, probably due to severe drought. Some people now believe they were descendants of the desert Archaic people who had occupied the area at places like High Rolls Cave and Fresnal Shelter.

The Jornada Mogollon homelands in the United States stretch from El Paso, Texas, in the south to near Carrizozo, New Mexico, and the Chupadera Mesa in the north and from the Rio Grande in the west to just past the Texas state line in the east.

Initially hunters by nature, while occupying the Three Rivers area, the Jornada Mogollon became farmers raising primarily corn, as evidenced by corncobs found at archaeological sites, and first lived in pithouses dug into the ground and with beams of sticks as roofs. Most faced the east. Floors were lined with rocks and plaster-like cysts. Pueblos were later built primarily of adobe as the result of better agriculture methods, allowing inhabitants to become sedentary. Some later pueblos also had community plaza areas. All

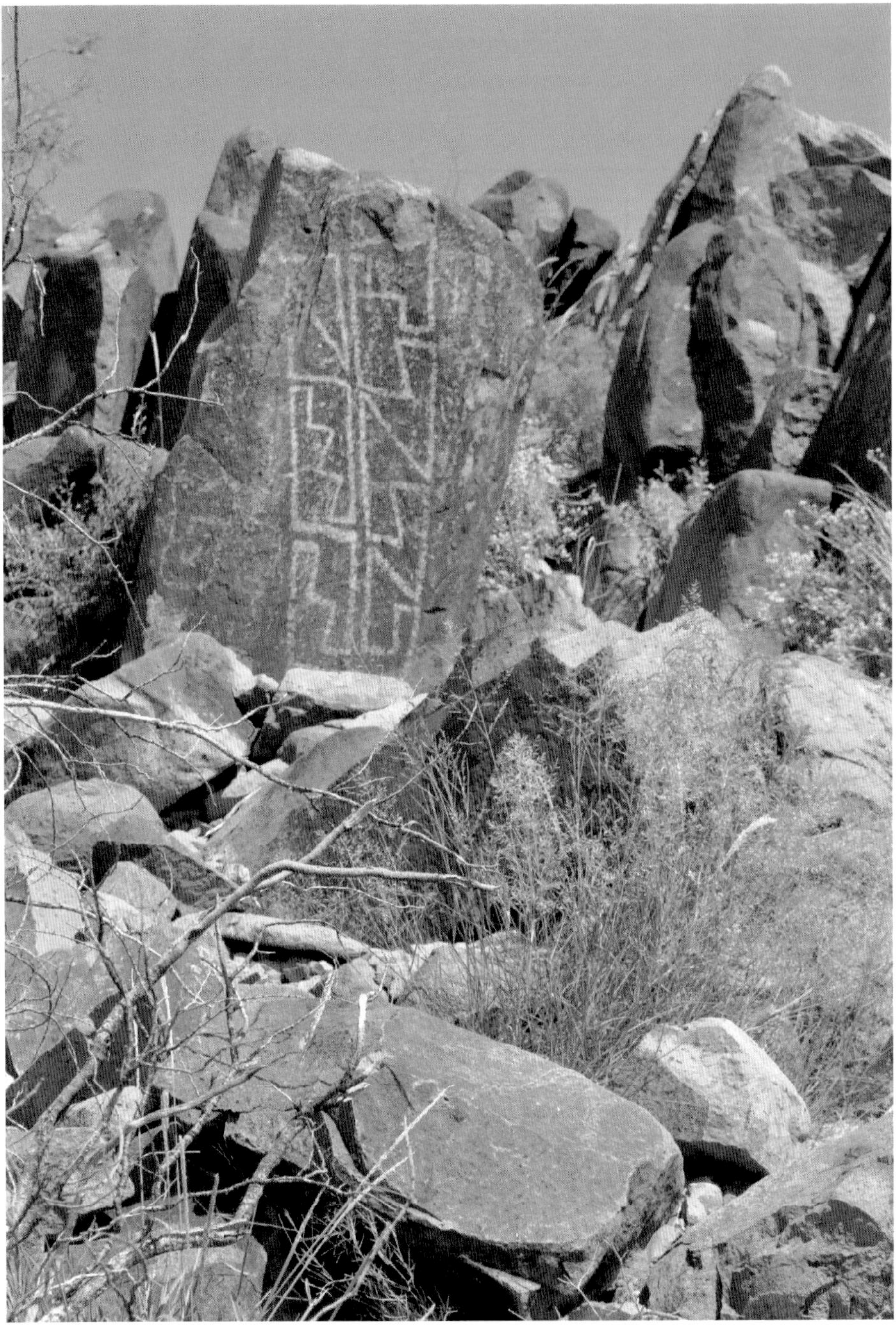

Geometric petroglyph at the Three Rivers Petroglyph Site. *Photo courtesy of Doyle Cozzens.*

these villages were established near permanent water sources—in this case, on or near Three Rivers.

Subsistence, based on archaeological evidence, included the primary hunted sources of deer and antelope, supplemented by sheep, elk and bear. Trapped animals were rabbit, squirrels, skunks and porcupines. Avian species hunted would have included quail, duck, doves and turkey. These meat sources would have been supplemented by acorns, piñon, yucca fruits, mesquite beans, cactus and wild fruit such as strawberries. Domesticated corn was also a staple.[3]

In what might be the first scholarly work on the Jornada Mogollon, Donald J. Lermer places their occupation into three phases. He postulates that during the Mesilla Phase, from AD 400 to 1150, the people lived in pithouses. The Early El Paso Phase, from AD 1150 to 1300, was characterized by pithouse and surface adobe structures. Local pottery included Chupadero black-on-white, Three Rivers red-on-terracotta, St. John's Polychrome and Lincoln black-on-red. During Lermer's final phase, the Late El Paso, from AD 1300 to 1450, pueblos consisted of room blocks, some with plaza areas. In addition to the pottery of the Early El Paso Phase, new types included Gila and Tonto Polychrome.[4]

Desert Jornada Mogollon

While Lerner identified three successive phases of Desert Jornada Mogollon—Mesilla, Dona Ana and the El Paso Phases—it is his Mesilla Phase (circa AD 400–1150) during which Three Rivers was inhabited, and small, dispersed settlements are thought to have been the norm.

Initially hunter-gatherers, the Three Rivers Jornada Mogollon probably did not begin domestic farming until circa AD 900. As these people settled into a routine of farming, they developed permanent villages with communal religious structures, began making pottery and started trading with other regional villages. Their major crops were beans, corn and squash.[5]

During the Mesilla Phase, the people lived in pithouses dug into the ground with a single family unit living in each pithouse. Even though they were farmers, much of their diet came from game and wild plants. Their pottery was a primitive brownware with little decoration. Late in the period, trade was begun with other sites.

During the Dona Ana Phase, pithouses were still used, but aboveground multi-room structures made of adobe and stone were beginning to be built.

There is some suggestion that these structures housed extended families. Local pottery became more decorative, and trade with other sites increased.

The El Paso Phase (AD 1150–1425) saw the widespread introduction of ceramic types such as Chupadero black-on-white, Three Rivers red-on-terracotta and Lincoln black-on-red. This phase is thought to have had a growing reliance on agriculture. Adobe room-block structures became the standard for this period, marked by a variety of ceramic types. Settlements became larger and more complex.[6]

By AD 1000, a thriving Jornada Mogollon community had developed in the Three Rivers Valley west of present-day Highway 54. For the next 350 years, village after village sprang up, only to be abandoned. Crops flourished, and the petroglyph (rock art) site was established. Built adjacent to the petroglyphs was Site 13, used for over 300 years as the home of some thirteen generations of Jornada Mogollon. For some unknown reason, Site 13 was abandoned around AD 1300. The Cosgrove Pueblo also flourished but was abandoned about AD 1350. Some of the occupants are thought to have migrated to the northeast around the Capitan Mountains as others might have migrated northwest, possibly as the ancient ancestors of today's pueblo people along the Rio Grande in northern New Mexico.

In 1977, Human Systems Research, Inc., conducted a detailed archaeological survey of the Three Rivers Valley and identified seven different periods of Jornada Mogollon occupation based on the various ceramic villages. The earliest occupants were farmers living on or near the creeks in Periods I and II. Period III began about AD 1150 with villages clustering around the petroglyphs and featured Chupadero black-on-white pottery. Period IV saw the decline of Mimbres pottery, and Period V saw introduction of Wingate black-on-red. During Periods IV and V, population decreased or villages combined, as only three villages were found. Periods IV and V saw the abandonment of two-thirds of the ceramic pueblos. During Period VI, decline continued as only Site 13 at the petroglyphs and one other site remained occupied. By Period VII, about AD 1300, only the Cosgrove Site remained occupied.[7]

Site abandonment began in AD 1120 and was mostly completed by AD 1350 with a few stragglers remaining until around AD 1450. Some of these people might have migrated north of the Capitan Mountains, while others, the ancestors of today's pueblo people, are thought to have migrated north and settled along the Rio Grande.

The Three Rivers group created one of the largest concentrations of petroglyphs in the United States, leaving over twenty-one thousand images

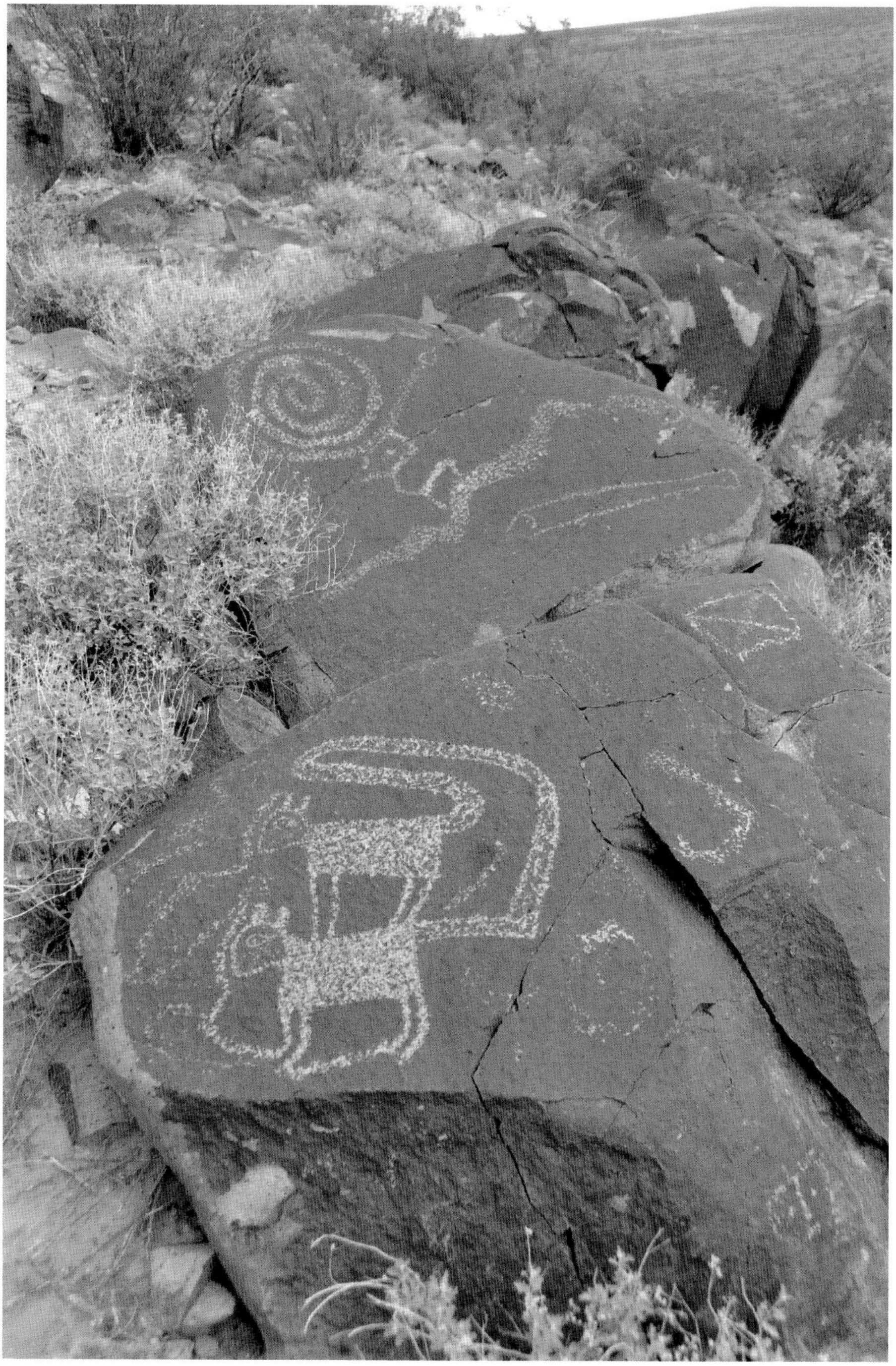

Petroglyphs of cats and snakes at the Three Rivers Petroglyph Site. *Photo courtesy of Margaret Berrier.*

within one square mile. The petroglyphs were either produced rapidly by scratching through the patina of the basalt rock or more permanently by using two rocks in the manner of a hammer and chisel to produce the design.

Prominent among the designs of the Three Rivers Mogollon was Tlaloc, a goggle-eyed rain god of Mesoamerica. Also prevalent were motifs, animals and geometrical shapes, especially circles with associated dots. Prevalent at the Three Rivers petroglyphs is the circle-and-dot motif.

In 1976, Human Systems Research, Inc., conducted the Three Rivers Drainage Archaeological Survey, a sample of the Three Rivers drainage from Sierra Blanca at twelve thousand feet above sea level to the floor of the Tularosa Basin at four thousand feet above sea level. The survey covered 277 square miles containing twenty-two quadrants measuring 0.5 by 1 mile. A total of sixty-six sites and seventy-one isolated occurrences were surveyed.[8]

The Three Rivers Petroglyph Site and Pueblo are listed on the State Register of Cultural Properties and consist of an "extensive selection of Archaic and Mogollon petroglyphs on a low hill and a pithouse surface pueblo village. No sites in the village are listed on the National Register of Historic Places."[9]

THE COSGROVE SITE AND REPORT[10]

In April 1925, Mr. and Mrs. C.B. Cosgrove and members of the El Paso Archaeological Society surveyed a Jornada Mogollon pueblo at Three Rivers. Senator Fall had given the group permission to survey and excavate any pueblos found on the ranch. The society's 1965 report, "Preliminary Survey of the El Paso Pueblo District," is more commonly referred to as the "Cosgrove Report."

From April 4 to April 17, the party excavated a ten-room block pueblo just to the east of the present-day Three Rivers railroad siding. Artifacts found at the site indicated that the pueblo was occupied about AD 1400.

After arriving at the site and meeting with Mrs. A.B. Fall, who offered quarters in one of the ranch's buildings, the party began surveying a potential site on the riverbank west of the ranch.

The party spent most of the second day examining a wonderful series of petroglyphs on the rim rock of one of the spurs of the Sierra Blanca Mountains. The foothill is one and a quarter miles northeast of Senator Fall's ranch home and extends in a northwesterly direction for at least three quarters of a mile. Nearly every boulder of the ridge is covered with

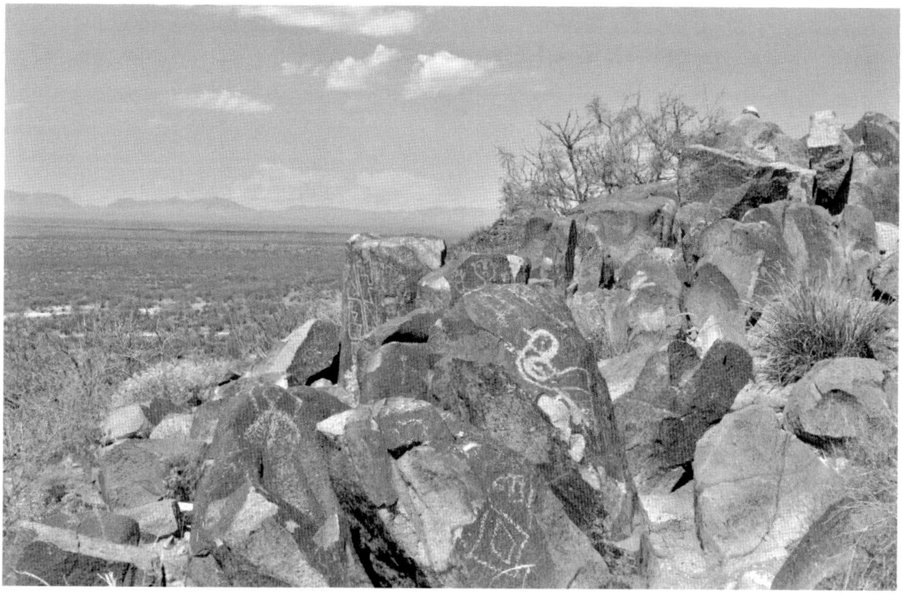

Petroglyph of bird and geometric shape with the San Andres Mountains in the background. *Photo courtesy of Doyle Cozzens.*

petroglyphs depicting symbolism and reptilian and animal life in all forms found in this sector.[11]

Two local laborers were hired, and work on the selected pueblo began on April 6. While excavating the first room, the skeletons of two adult females were uncovered. Over the next eleven days, the pueblo was excavated and facts noted, such as that the walls were ten inches thick and that corners in the structure seldom varied from ninety-degree angles. Typical artifacts such as decayed posts and pottery were discovered.

April 16 was the last day for archaeology, and the final report noted:

> *Of the ten rooms excavated, two were accidentally burned leaving the remains of posts and vigas. The other eight rooms had not been consumed by fire and were barren of timbers. This leads to believe that the pueblo was abandoned and robbed of its roof timbers when the migration took place to another and possibly more protected site. Outside doors at one time opened and at a later period sealed with rocks, as discovered by excavation, also suggests troubled times, followed by a movement of the people to a safer location.*
>
> *The permanent buildings and the finding of corn cobs proves that these people were agriculturalists and therefore Pueblo Indians.*[12]

Two rooms were burned, and two more rooms had subfloor burials. Subsequent surveys indicated more rooms below the ridge that were not noted by the Cosgrove party. Tree ring and pottery dating place site occupation at AD 1425.

In 1977, archaeologists Mark Wimberly and Alan Rogers returned to the Cosgrove Site for additional excavations. They recorded nine room blocks separated on the south side of the Three Rivers drainage. The foundation of the pueblo was constructed of large river cobbles (in some cases adobe) and was jacal-like in structure.

In addition to the Cosgrove Site, Wimberley and Rogers discovered eight additional sites, each consisting of a small house block. If the Cosgroves discovered these additional sites, they were not recorded. The site is not readily recognizable today due to excavations, erosion, pot hunting and having been bulldozed.[13]

The pueblo was abandoned around AD 1350 and might well have been the last occupied site before the Jornada Mogollon abandoned the area for good.

The Three Rivers Pueblo

In 1976, archaeologists from New Mexico State University excavated a pueblo across the road from the Three Rivers Petroglyph Site. Named the Three Rivers Site, it consisted of a masonry surface structure; a multi-room, semi-subsurface adobe structure; a group of storage bins; and a living surface. There were perhaps fifteen to twenty households at the site (or fifty to seventy people) during each of the twelve generations.

Although the village was small compared to other sites in New Mexico, it was large for the Three Rivers region. And while its inhabitants farmed along the river, they were still dependent on hunting and gathering wild food. As the village expanded, it extended eastward and became less dependent on hunting and gathering and more dependent on farming. Around AD 1200, trade with other sites in the Southwest and Mexico became more important, and the nearby petroglyph site was made. The site reached its greatest importance by AD 1300 but was abandoned by AD 1400.[14]

Occupied from circa AD 900 to AD 1350, it was the longest-used pueblo in the area. Once abandoned, its occupants moved downstream to the Cosgrove Pueblo or other similar sites:

The masonry structure was a single, rectangular semi-subterranean room with four post supports and two small, additional posts. The roof had burned. The adobe structure consisted of four rooms, three of which were excavated. The walls were built of coarse adobe over a level gypsum layer. Two of the rooms were roughly square; the third rectangular with rounded corners. All rooms contained hearths and posthole; some had stone ground artifacts and some, burials. Four storage pots were evacuated. The structures were probably roofed when they were in use.[15]

Three Rivers Petroglyph Site

Without a doubt, the most important Jornada site in the Three Rivers area is the Three Rivers Petroglyph Site and Pueblo, currently administered by the Bureau of Land Management.

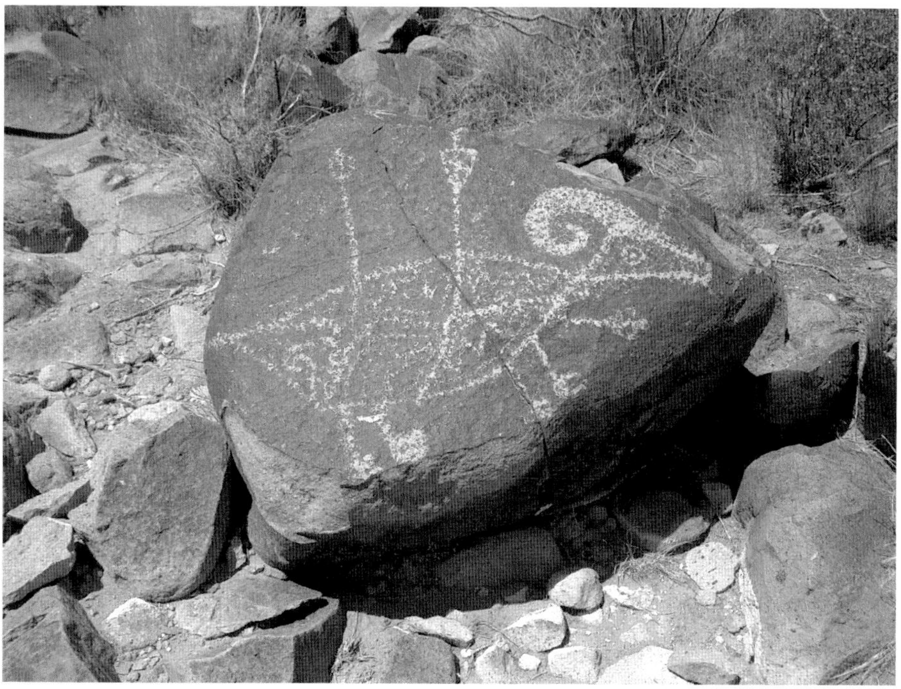

This bighorn sheep is probably the most photographed petroglyph at the Three Rivers Petroglyph Site. *Photo courtesy of Carl Jenkins.*

Arguably the most prevalent rock art style in New Mexico is that of the Jornada Mogollon. Polly Schaafsma places the emergence of rock art at Three Rivers at AD 1000, comparing the rock arts to the similarities of Mimbres black-on-white ceramics. She also suggests that the petroglyphs and Three Rivers Pueblo are linked in a socio-religious sense.[16]

Archaeological research indicates that these sites were probably occupied by the Jornada Mogollon from about AD 750 to 1200. The petroglyphs are located on a basalt ridge 1.5 miles long, running from southeast to northwest. The ridge rises 280 feet above the surrounding plain. The height of the ridge is 4,985 feet above sea level. There are at least 20,824 petroglyphs and 559 graffiti recorded at the site. By comparison, the Petroglyph National Monument located in Albuquerque contains 20,000 glyphs. The "West Knoll" lies immediately west of the main trail and also has an impressive number of petroglyphs.

The Cosgrove party visited the site in 1925, but perhaps the first person to formally survey it was Herbert Yeo in 1953. Yeo "chalked" and photographed 102 images. Sometime following at an unknown date, the Chaves County Archaeological Society recorded 767 petroglyphs. The El Paso Archaeological Society returned in 1973 and recorded 468 petroglyphs found in the first nine hundred feet of the site. A second major recording effort by the El Paso Archaeological Society was led by archaeologist Helen Crotty in May 1975. This was followed by Human Systems Research, Inc., in 1976.

The true nature and meaning of the petroglyphs are unknown. It is generally accepted that the petroglyphs are probably secular; some even postulate that many might be clan symbols. General shapes at Three Rivers include anthropomorphic, zoomorphic (birds, fish and fish-men, which predominate the site) and general/abstract (circle motif). Clan symbols suggested include the parrot (X) and bear (bear paw).

There is also an abundance of horned animals, turtles and lizards. Circles with dots, both inside and out, are frequent. Another frequent motif at Three Rivers is the swastika. Most Mogollon swastikas face counterclockwise, but those at this site face clockwise.

Perhaps the best description of Jornada Mogollon rock comes from Polly Schaafsma, the preeminent rock art expert in New Mexico:

> *Like Mimbres pottery designs, Jornada Style rock art is characterized by life-forms, frequently delineated in outline with emphasis on heads that are shown with facial features. Rock art elements include a variety of highly stylized animals, birds, horned serpents, trapezoidal or rectangular figures with huge eyes, both naturalistic and formalized anthropomorphs, and faces*

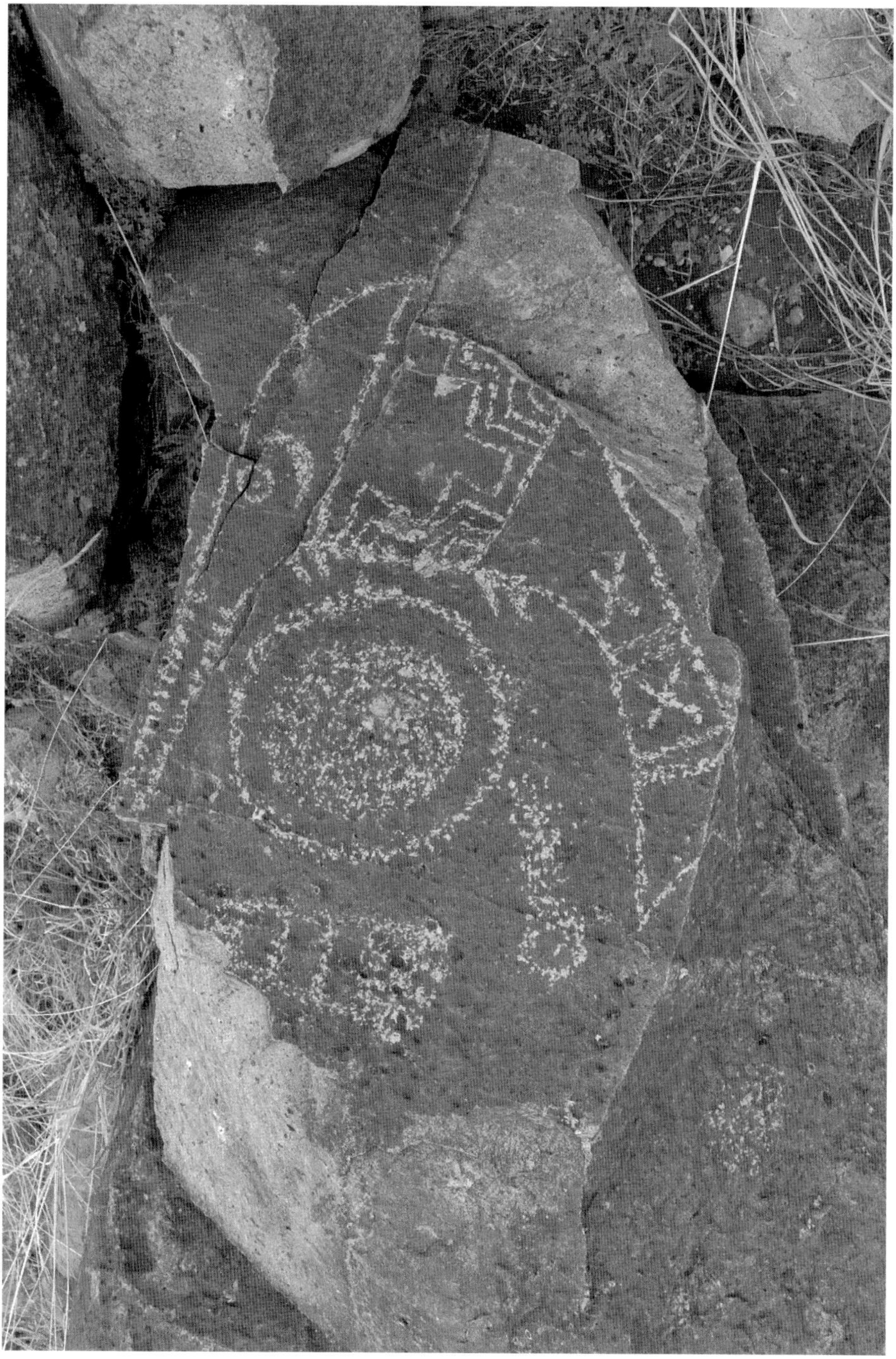

Petroglyph of head and bear claw. *Photo courtesy of Margaret Berrier.*

> *and masks as independent elements. In addition there are cloud terraces with rainbows at the base and large formal abstracts that incorporate step frets and mazelike elements, some of which represent textile or pottery designs.*[17]

There was no actual habitation on the petroglyph site. Nearby at the Three Rivers Pueblo, however, the lack of masks usually associated with religious sites suggests, although debatably, that the site might have been used for secular rather than religious ceremonies. One prominent archaeologist, Joe Ben Sanders of Tularosa, proposes the story of the mythical Battle of Casa Grandes starts with Bureau of Land Management Marker 5 and includes four hundred petroglyphs.

Interpretation of the rock art is controversial at best. Best theories support the linkage of the Three Rivers site with worship of the Mexican deities Tlaloc and Quetzalcoatl. Perhaps the best interpretation of the petroglyphs is contained in Polly Schaafsma's *Rock Art in New Mexico*. A more aggressive interpretation is provided in the works of Joe Ben Sanders (listed in the bibliography), who definitely provides an interpretation of the petroglyphs and likens them to modern-day Hopi People.[18]

One last group of rock images are modern graffiti, including names, dates and the like, which makes up 5.6 percent of the site.

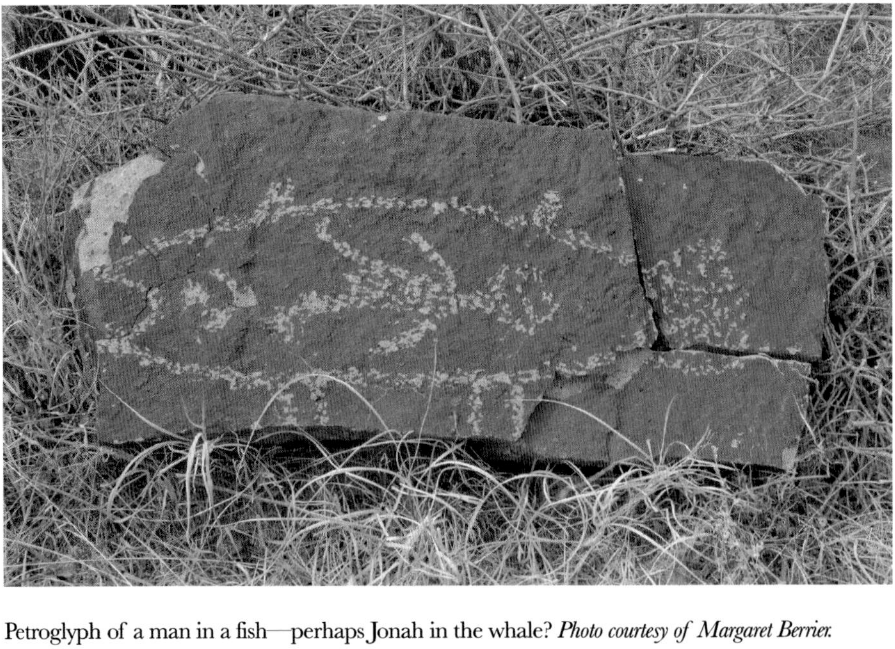

Petroglyph of a man in a fish—perhaps Jonah in the whale? *Photo courtesy of Margaret Berrier.*

Hatchet Site

Perhaps one of the earliest Jornada Mogollon sites in the Three Rivers Valley was located adjacent to the Hatchet Ranch. In 1961, Eugene McCluney published a report describing the excavation of the Hatchet Site across Highway 54 from the Three Rivers Trading Post. In his report, McCluney described pithouse rooms as circular, rectangular or square with entrances on top of the pithouses.[19] The site was further described by Mark Wimberly and Alan Rogers in 1977 as a large Mogollon village on the alluvial plain overlooking Three Rivers Creek where it entered the Tularosa Basin. The study found that the site extended over a mile long and that the ruins continued to the north to a position near the Hatchet Ranch.[20]

Three Rivers Red-on-Terracotta Pottery

While many pottery types are found in the Three Rivers area, one is unique: Three Rivers red-on-terracotta. It is the second type in the general category of Three Rivers redware series and was the most widely traded and easily recognized of ceramics. Named by C.B. Cosgrove, the Three Rivers red-on-terracotta was primarily, if not solely, produced in the Sacramento Mountains area. H.P. Mera wrote:

> *Its headquarters, Mr. Cosgrove believes, is at and about Three Rivers, New Mexico, east of the Rio Grande. It occurs, however, in the form of sherds in a great many Mimbres sites.*[21]

2

The Mescalero Apaches

After the abandonment of the area by the Jornada Mogollon, the next known inhabitants were the Mescalero Apaches. Several accounts describe nomadic Indians, presumably early Apache groups, within the historic Mescalero range in the 1500s and 1600s. By the mid-1700s, Spanish accounts commonly identified such inhabitants as Mescaleros, meaning "mescal eaters."

By the time of the Spanish colonization of New Mexico in the mid-seventeenth century, Mescalero Apaches had established themselves in the mountains east of the Rio Grande. The Spaniards recorded conflicts with local Apaches as early as 1653, when the latter reportedly raided the Jumano Pueblo of Gran Quivira. Juan Dominguez led a retaliatory expedition against adjacent Apaches living in the Sierra Blanca area. For the next two centuries, the Mescaleros were often in conflict with Europeans and other native tribes.[22]

Early Apaches sustained themselves by hunting and gathering. As Spanish (and later Anglo) contact increased, they survived by transitioning to trading, limited agriculture and raiding. Agriculture consisted of planting corn and wheat in small plots and leaving fields mostly untended throughout the growing season. After the 1870s, the Apaches were also growing watermelons, cantaloupes, chilis, beans, pumpkins, squash and potatoes. Trade gave them corn, blankets, flour, sugar, salt, iron kettles and clothing in exchange for buffalo hides, meat and lard.[23]

Shelters were categorized as *rancherías* (a group of structures). Most shelters were temporary or seasonal, and almost nothing remains of these sites.

Frameworks were made of wooden poles and branches with hides sometimes placed over them. Kilns used in preparing mescal were also common. For the Mescalero Apaches, storage was critical to their survival during winter and into the summer growing season.

In the 1850s, the Sierra Blanca Apaches tried to avoid contact with the Americans and stayed within their territory. But the American government continually decreased their hunting and gathering range, thus increasing the necessity of raiding. In 1852, Governor William C. Lane signed a treaty with the Mescaleros, providing rations for five years, but the government did not honor the treaty. By 1854, raiding had become prevalent throughout southeastern New Mexico, and at that time there were as many as twenty-six leaders of the tribe. As a result, Governor David Meriwether intensified military actions against the Apaches, with Fort Stanton established in 1855 to maintain control of the Mescalero Apaches. The Apaches ceased raiding, and a large band under Cadette settled near Fort Stanton that year.

After being abandoned in 1861 due to the Confederate invasion of New Mexico, Fort Stanton was reoccupied in 1862, and resulting forays forced the Mescaleros to surrender. They were interned at Bosque Redondo near present-day Fort Sumner, and by 1863, more than four hundred Apaches were living at the Bosque. But the presence of their enemy, the Navajos, at the Bosque caused many Apaches to desert and revert to raiding. Most eventually returned to the Sierra Blanca area.[24]

An executive order on May 29, 1873, established the present Mescalero Reservation. By the time the Europeans came into the area following the Civil War, the Three Rivers area abutted the Mescalero Reservation on the western side.

While most of the Mescaleros now live on the main part of the reservation south and east of Sierra Blanca, there is a small settlement northwest of the reservation known as the Shanta Community.

Marilyn Cozzens, who lived at Three Rivers with her parents in the 1950s, commented:

> *There were three houses of Shantas at Three Rivers* [in the 1940s]. *Joe Shanta was in charge, and there were five families that lived up there and they had about ten kids. One of the other families was Virginia* [Shanta] *and Bruce Klinecole, and they had three kids. She became president of the Mescalero Apache Tribe. Bruce was very industrious. He grew alfalfa and sold to Tom Ryan and Carroll Johnson. They were always nicely*

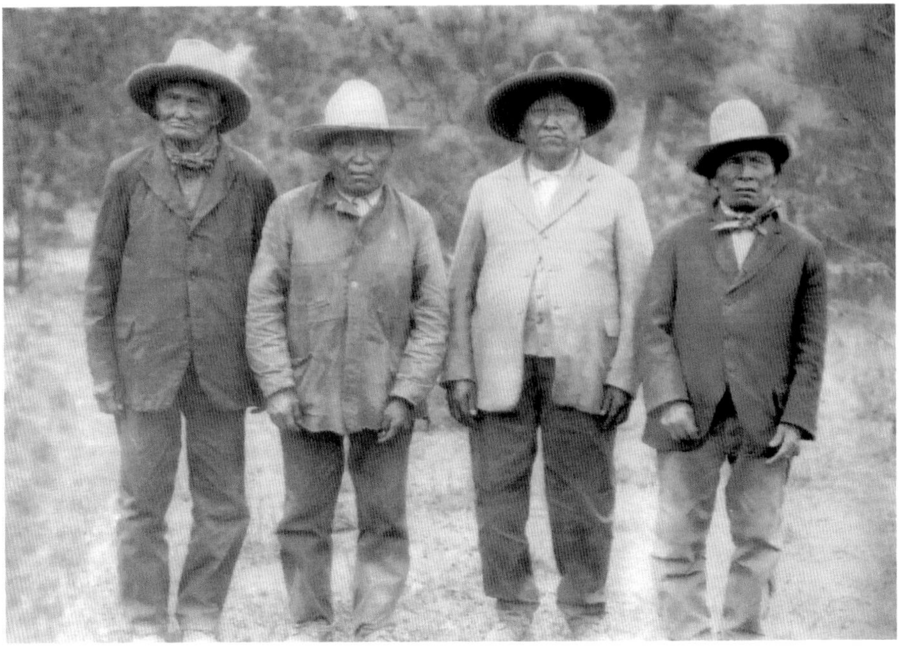

Photograph of (left to right) Harold Dick, Joe Behetta, Shanta Boy and Ishpia, taken at Three Rivers. *Photo courtesy of Pamela Blagg.*

> *dressed, and Virginia had very good command of English and was a good communicator. All of these kids went to school with us.*[25]

Shanta Boy was the leader of the Shanta community when it was established on the west side of Sierra Blanca, probably in the 1870s. As an orphan raised by nonrelatives, and following the Apache custom of the time, he was given his father's name followed by "Boy."

Shanta Boy herded sheep, as did almost all Mescaleros of the time. He gradually added sheep to his herd on the range near Rinconada, but during the winter months, he and his family drove them down the western slope of Sierra Blanca. As time went by, the Shanta family built a small community on the west side of the mountain. Being in close proximity to Tularosa, the Shantas were able to hire workers to help them with their sheep as their herd grew. At one time, Shanta Boy was reported to have had five thousand sheep, some cattle and horses. With his sons' help, he raised corn, beans, pumpkins and squash.[26]

As a young man, Shanta Boy was reported to have participated in attacks on stagecoaches on their route between El Paso and Mesilla. There are also stories of a murder on his place, possibly due to bootlegged alcohol or *tiswin*,[27] a fermented drink the Apache made. Shanta Boy was convicted of the murder and sent to prison at Fort Leavenworth, Kansas. After being imprisoned there for a while, he and a few others escaped.[28]

One day, Shanta Boy and four others escaped prison by going through the wire at the end of the day. Pursued by guards and bloodhounds, the Mescaleros ran until overtaken by the bloodhounds, at which time Choneska, who was said to have power over dogs, "annexed" the dogs and took them along with the escapees. The guards could not figure out what happened; they knew only that the dogs went silent.

The Apaches traveled west toward Sierra Blanca, avoiding discovery along the way while finding clothes and food. Finally reaching the Mescalero Reservation, the group, along with the dogs, hid at Rinconada.

Once they reached the reservation, they were warned by other Mescaleros that they were being pursued by guards and laid low until the guards left. They knew that although they were registered on the reservation, very few people there would recognize them.[29]

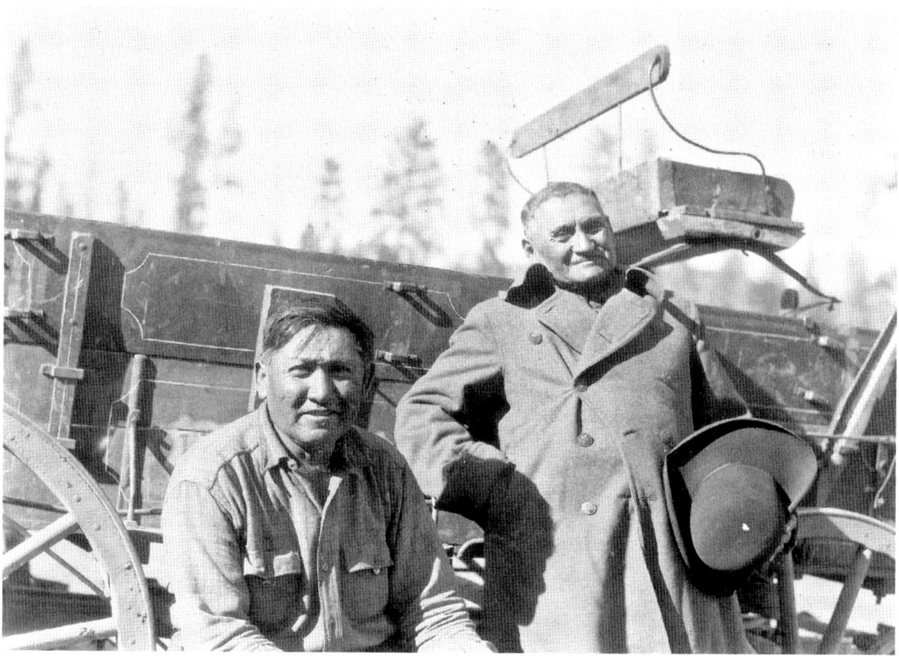

Ralph Shanta (seated) and Joe Shanta at the Three Rivers Shanta community on the Mescalero Apache Reservation. *Photo courtesy New Mexico State University Library, Archives and Special Collections, Image 00080010.*

J. Denton Simms, whose family homesteaded near the Shanta community, tells of dealing with Shanta Boy:

> *Those Apaches who visited us at Three Rivers came from a nearby camp whose head man was called Shanta. We learned that Shanta and his community had been coming to our ranch for many years because our predecessors had given them fruit as it began to ripen in the small orchard. We were glad to continue the custom not only because we had surplus fruit, but also because we were happy to have this means of making friends with the Indians. Little did I suspect, then, that I would be spending many, many years working with Apaches.*[30]

Simms's father, a doctor, spent time helping the Mescaleros. Even though the reservation had its own doctor located only twenty-five miles away, intervening were two mountain ridges, and getting to the doctor required a circuitous trip over many miles. The Mescalero used traditional healing in many cases, but for cases with broken bones or other emergencies, they came to Dr. Simms.

When Simms saved a woman's life after a breech birth, local Apaches gave him a horse for his daughter Mary, and the reservation administration sent him a check for $100 in appreciation.[31]

Among the more prominent members of the Shanta family was Virginia Shanta Klinecole, first tribal chair of the Mescalero Apache Tribe. When Virginia was born on June 13, 1924, her mother developed complications, and Father Braun was sent for to administer the last rites of the Catholic Church. Upon arrival, Father Braun declared that the baby would live and helped the mother to survive also.

As Virginia grew up, she became a favorite of Father Braun. Starting at the age of two, he would take her riding with him strapped to his back as they rode the horse. He followed her activities with pride as she progressed through school. Initially, she worked at the Tularosa Schools as Mescalero Tribal Liaison.[32]

During World War II, Father Braun was captured in the Philippine Islands and spent the remainder of the war in a Japanese prisoner of war camp. One of the other prisoners was Bruce Klinecole, a Kiowa-Apache, also from New Mexico. While in the Philippines, Klinecole was told of Virginia and vowed that if he survived the war, he would marry her. When the war ended, both men returned to Mescalero.[33]

After returning from the war, Bruce Klinecole arrived at Mescalero and was converted to Catholicism by Father Braun. It was there that

Father Braun married Bruce and Virginia. Bruce fell in love with Three Rivers, as Virginia remembered:

> *Bruce was in and out of Oklahoma before we were married, but of course we stayed here in Mescalero afterward. He was a ranch lover—he loved horses and cattle. That's my love too. We rode horseback together, he and I, we herded cattle together, we had our children and ranched together. And my husband was very insistent that our four children were baptized.*[34]

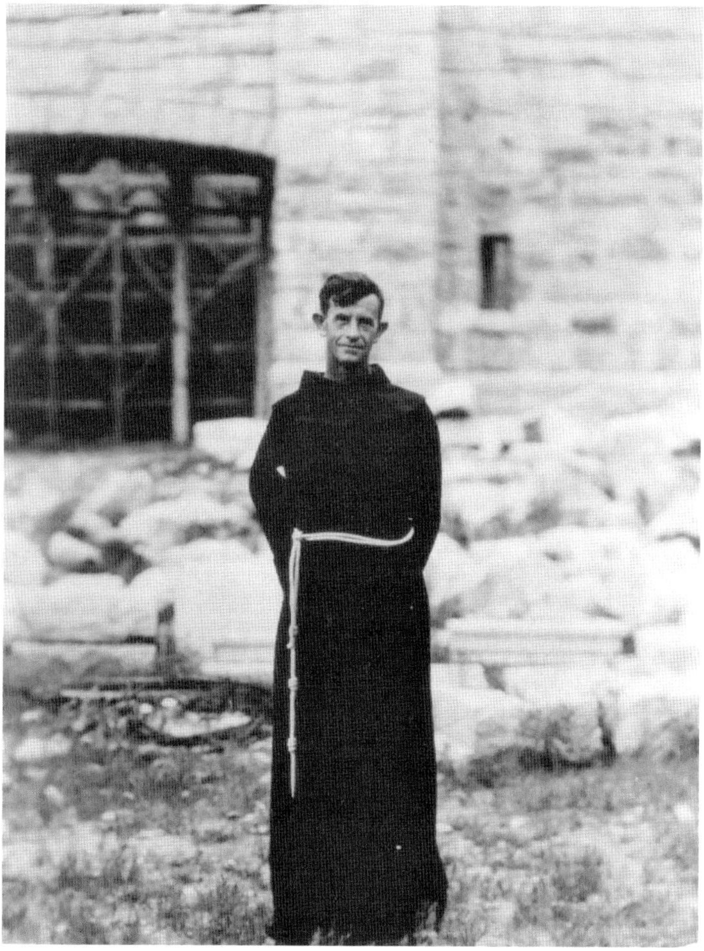

Photograph of Father Albert Braun in front of the Saint Joseph's Mission, Mescalero, circa 1925. *Photo courtesy of Mary Serna, St. Joseph Apache Mission Collection.*

Shortly thereafter, Virginia was elected to the Mescalero Tribal Council, serving for over thirty years, and later became chair of the tribe in 1959, the first woman elected to such a position in the United States. She died on March 13, 2011.

Though not a member of the Mescalero Apache Tribe, Father Albert Braun, a Franciscan monk from Los Angeles, had a close association with Three Rivers. Father Braun was first sent to the Mescalero Apache Reservation in 1916 to minister to the needs of the people. As he established himself at Mescalero, he became fond of the Shanta community at Three Rivers.

Once a month, Father Braun tried to say Mass at the Shanta community, but to get there he had to travel more than forty miles through Tularosa rather than the ten or so miles across Sierra Blanca. To get to the Shanta Rancheria, Braun had to ride past the Fall Ranch. On Braun's first trip to Three Rivers, he left Tularosa at dawn with Father Ferdinand, hoping to avoid the midday heat. Braun fell in love with the region and promised to come back often.

Virginia Shanta Klinecole described Father Albert:

> *He traveled straight across Mescalero, which is about thirty miles by horseback over the mountain. He would stop at every Apache camp and stay overnight with them, share a meal, and then start to the next camp, all the way back to Three Rivers. He'd come over the hill on horseback, and he'd get with my grandfather…They were very strong friends, and he'd always stay with us, maybe a couple of days, and say mass every day. That's the reason most of my family are Catholic—because of Father Al.*
>
> *That's the kind of person he was. He was with the people…He didn't say, "Well, here is a catechism, we're going to learn about Catholic religion." He was a man of God…a true Franciscan. He didn't care whether someone was another religion—he wanted them to know about God…and he visited families—Baptist or Dutch Reform or whatever. He'd go in and visit, share a meal, talk.*[35]

On a subsequent trip, Albert Fall noticed Braun riding by and sent his daughter Jouett to bring the priest to his ranch. Not only did Fall ask Father Braun to spend the night, but he also offered his house whenever Braun came to the area, an offer the priest gratefully accepted. From that point forward, Father Braun and the Falls became close friends.[36]

As time went on, Father Braun decided that a chapel was needed at the Shanta community, even though there was no money to build it. About the time he returned from being a witness at the Albert Fall Teapot Dome trial, Braun received word from Monsignor Hughes, director of the Marquette League (an organization that helped Indian missions), that two wealthy young women from New York wished to donate $2,000 to build a new chapel. The church was to be named Saints Patrick and Brigid in honor of their parents.

Father Hughes approached Father Bonaventure Oblasser proposing that the money offered for the church should be sent to Arizona instead to build a school. When the donors protested, the money reverted to Three Rivers, but the sisters stipulated the building was to be of stone and have stained-glass windows.

While $2,000 was a good start, it was far short of the amount needed to construct the building. Father Braun approached Shanta Boy, who thought about what was required. Finally, he went back to Father Braun and informed the priest that he would help build the chapel. Together, Shanta Boy and Father Braun found a suitable place to build the chapel.

When Shanta Boy asked Father Braun what the chapel was to be named, the padre replied, "Saint Patrick," dropping the name Brigid. Shanta Boy did not like the name and therefore refused to supply the land. At that point, Braun suggested San Patricio, which Shanta Boy liked. The land was provided, and plans to build the church began.

Shanta Boy knew the location of good rocks that could be used to construct the chapel. Material was available to make the lime and logs for the interior of the building. With a wagon and team to haul materials to the site, other locals offered help constructing the building.

Work began in November, and the chapel was completed by Christmas. With the construction begun, the next task was to procure stained-glass windows. Friends of Father Braun's in St. Louis found a church being torn down that had stained-glass windows that had been made in Europe and were available for a reasonable price. With the exterior of the building completed, work turned to furnishing the interior. The pews and altar were constructed of native lumber hand-hewn onsite.

Virginia Klinecole, a small girl at the time, told of the building of the chapel:

> *All helped each other. Hispanics, Apaches—they were all together building that chapel. My grandfather—he had a herd of goats, and I guess he provided the feeding of the people as they were building. I remember the female members of my family preparing the meals. The neighbors all came. They were there bringing food—chile or beans or tortillas or whatever—and my grandfather provided the meat. They all had open fires and they cooked.*

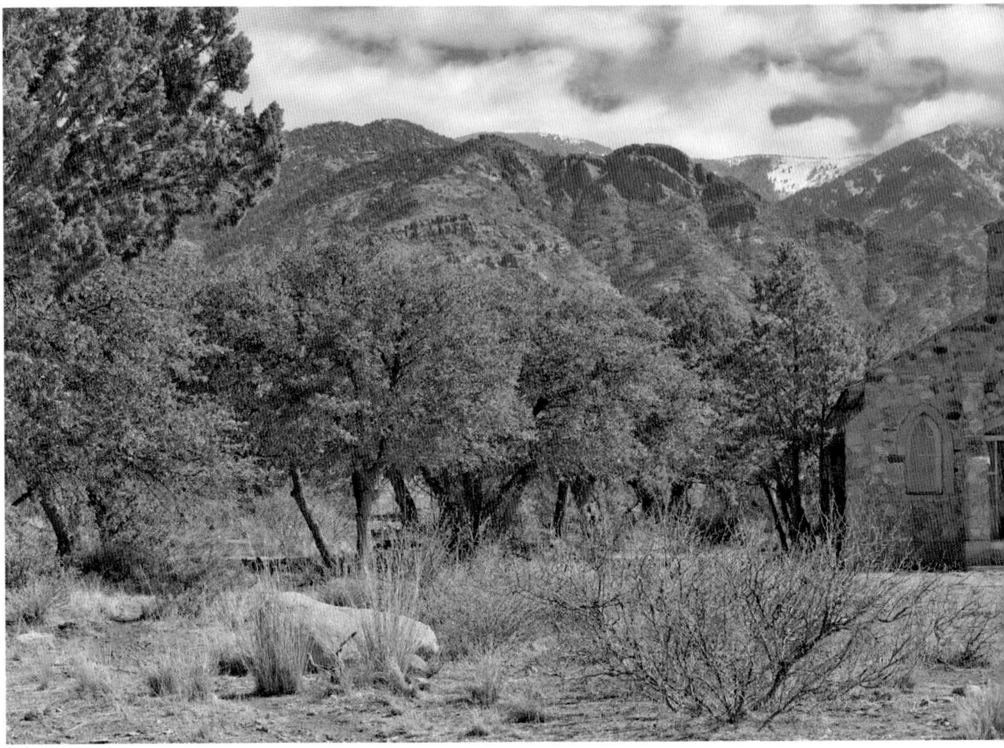

San Patricio Chapel at the Shanta community, built by the Shanta Boy family, neighbors and Father Albert Braun. *Photo courtesy of Richard T. Bryant.*

> *And they would eat together and then go back to work again. Daylight to dark. It was a unified effort.*[37]

Braun completed San Patricio Chapel at a cost of $1,990 and sent a report and a money order for $10 to Monsignor Hughes. Return mail found a $100 donation from the Monsignor.[38]

During World War II, Father Braun went to the Philippine Islands with the 200th Coast Artillery of the New Mexico National Guard. Captured, he spent the war in a Japanese prisoner of war camp administering to the needs of the prisoners. After the war, he returned to Mescalero but was soon assigned posts in other states. After his death on March 6, 1983, he was buried in St. Joseph's sanctuary, the only non-Mescalero to be buried on the reservation.

The other prominent member of the Shanta community was Sarah Misquez, who was also tribal president. Born on September 6, 1945,

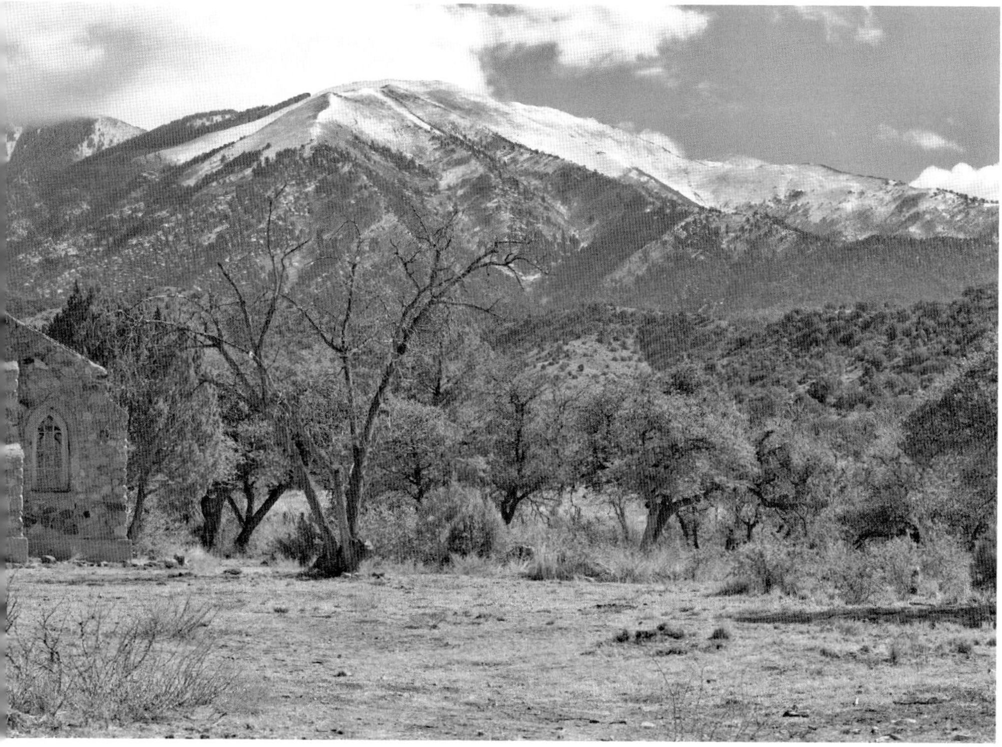

Misquez earned a degree in business from Haskell Indian Nations University in Lawrence, Kansas. She married Gilbert Misquez and served as the tribe's administrator, council member and tribal secretary.

Misquez was first appointed tribal president in May 1999 following the death of Wendell Chino on May 4, 1998, and the ouster of Paul Ortega in May 1999. A longtime aide of Chino's, Misquez won election in August 1999 but was defeated by Chino's son Mark in the subsequent election in 2001. However, the results were thrown out due to a voting controversy, and she won a special election in January 2002. She defeated Chino again in November 2003 but was herself defeated by Carleton Naiche-Palmer in 2007.

Misquez died in a one-car accident on Highway 70 near Tularosa on January 9, 2008, when the car she was driving veered into the median and overturned. She was survived by her husband, two sons and one daughter.

G.L. Tucker grew up with the Shanta community. He remembers:

Mescalero Community was mainly comprised of the Shantas, Bigropes and Klinecoles. Bruce Klinecole had a pretty good orchard and hay fields. Virginia Klinecole was president of the Mescalero Apache Tribe for a while as was Sarah Misquez who was raised there. She was Ralph Shanta's daughter. Joe Shanta's son Charley [would] *come down to store and hitch a ride to Tularosa. We meet each other on street and roll up sleeves like* [we were] *going to fight and then shake hands.*[39]

3

Patrick Coghlan, Billy the Kid and Susan McSween Barber

The Europeans Come

While the Spanish *entrada* into New Mexico began with the expedition of Francisco Vasquez de Coronado in 1540, it appears their first excursion into the Three Rivers area occurred in the fall of 1765. In January of that year, Pedro Jose de Fuente assumed the billet of captain of the Presidio of El Paso. Faced by hit-and-run attacks by Mescalero Apaches, he formed a punitive expedition under the command of Alferez Jose Patricio Lucero to penetrate the Sacramento Mountains and attack the Mescaleros in their homeland.

Lucero's army of 239 men departed El Paso the night of September 17 to hide the dust of their column. Initially traveling up the Rio Grande, the army turned east and on the twentieth was passing through the White Sands. The next morning, they reached the area near present-day Alamogordo, where they found an Apache camp. It was obvious the Spaniards had been discovered.

Although it is thought they moved north near La Luz, it is possible that the excursion reached an area just south of Three Rivers. Lucero described the land as suitable for agriculture because of its nature and the abundance of springs, providing plenty of water for irrigation. The Spaniards followed the Mescaleros to an area thick with tule, rockrose, *gardunales* and cottonwoods.

Lucero and his men departed the area on September 23 and returned to El Paso on September 27, taunted by the Mescaleros all the way.

Ten years later, the Spanish were ready for their next excursion into the Sacramento Mountains, this time under the command of Don Hugo O'Conor, an Irish exile. O'Conor had been named the commandant inspector for New Spain.

O'Conor devised a plan for four columns to converge on the Sacramento Mountains. Jose Antonio de Arrieta, lieutenant governor of New Mexico, led a force north from El Paso through the Organ Mountains and east to Sierra Blanca, a route that took him north of the White Sands toward Three Rivers. Eventually, all four columns met in the Sacramento Mountains and skirmished with the Mescaleros. By December of that year, O'Conor and his forces had returned to El Paso.[40]

While the exact routes of these early expeditions are unknown, circumstantial evidence points to the Three Rivers area. A thirteenth-century Limoges cross made of copper with enamel was found by Albert Fall's son-in-law, Mahlon Everhart, in a ditch bank near the Fall House. Three inches long, it was thought to have belonged to a Catholic priest.[41]

A second intriguing artifact eroded from a small dune in the area was the remnant of an eighteenth-century Spanish flintlock musket consisting of the barrel, forearm strap, lock plate and small fragments of brass parts. No other related evidence of a Spanish presence was found.[42]

THE EUROPEAN SETTLERS ARRIVE

The original village of Three Rivers was settled around 1862 about four miles east of its current site. Following the Battle of Round Mountain in 1868, from the 1870s to the 1890s, many other families arrived to settle in the Three Rivers area, most of them Hispanic.

The first settlers in the area were thought to have been the Armijo family (possibly from Socorro). According to Victorino Crawford, born in the area about 1875, two Armijo families built houses in the Three Rivers area. One was in the lower river valley near Jack Fall Spring (later the site of Albert Fall's son Jack's house), and the other was at the confluence of the three rivers near the south bank of Indian Creek. Both sites were abandoned shortly thereafter, although the Indian Creek site was later used intermittently.[43]

At the time of the Armijos or shortly thereafter, other settlers, including Andresio Padilla, Juan Padilla and Rumaldo Martinez, arrived and started homes and ranches. Early efforts centered on the raising of sheep, goats and

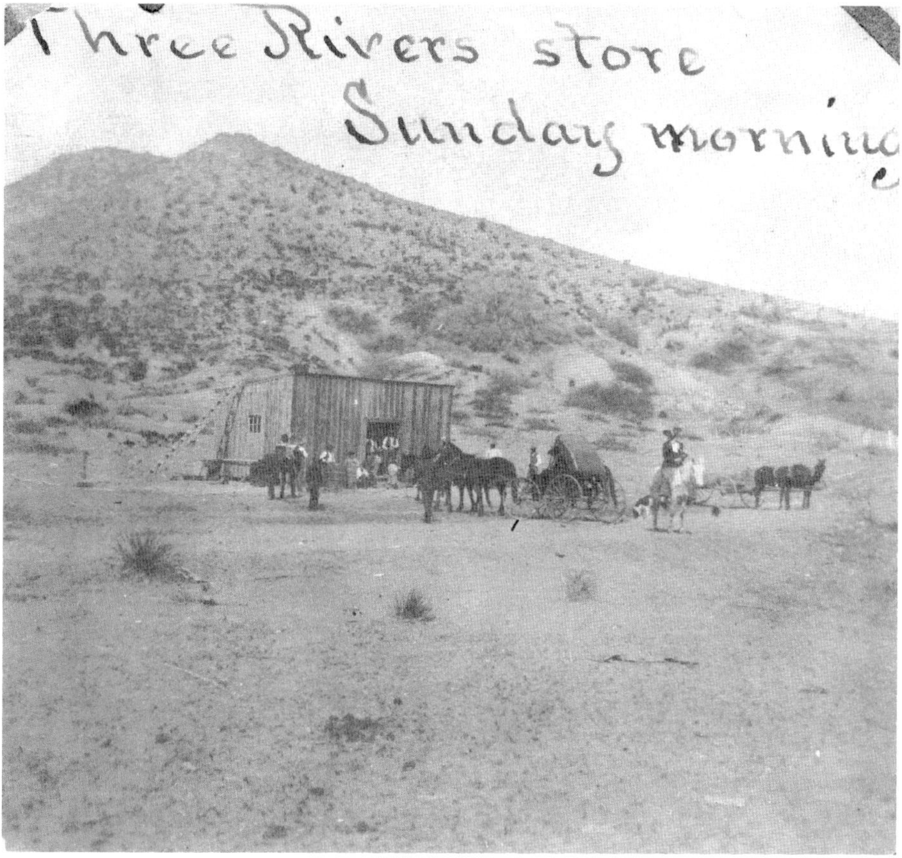

Three Rivers Store on Sunday morning, circa 1940. *Photo courtesy of Tularosa Basin Historical Society, Image P319.*

some cattle. A limited number of hand-dug wells were also built. Ditches were dug on the south side of Indian Creek and northeast of Three Rivers Creek. Small farms were established in the bottomlands, and a few springs were improved to provide water for stock as well as to irrigate small farms popping up in the basin.[44]

One of the prominent families to settle in the area at that time was the Andalecio and Paublita Marino Padilla family, who migrated to the Three Rivers area from Las Padillas. One daughter, Candelaria, was born there in 1897. Andalecio was loaned cattle from his uncle Don Pomozeno Marino to start his Three Rivers ranch. Coming with the Andalecio Padilla family to Three Rivers were his parents, Juan and Rosalia Chavez Padilla. Juan (1810–1898) and Rosalia (1821–1899) are buried in the Three Rivers Cemetery.

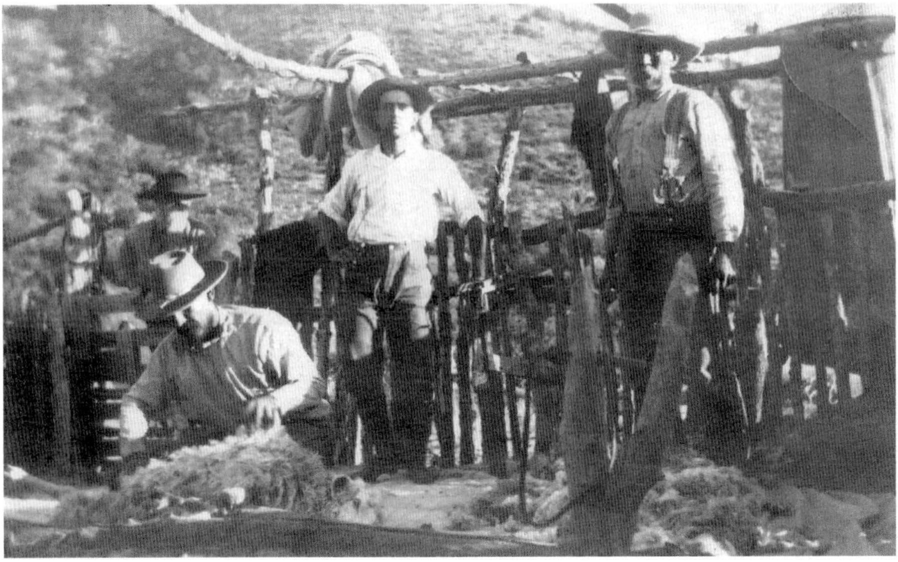

Sheep shearing, circa 1940. *Photo courtesy of Tularosa Basin Historical Society, Image P321.*

The Padillas' daughter, Candelaria, born at Three Rivers in February 1879, married Felipe Sanchez from Hondo.

Among the early settlers was Dona Lucas, mother of Victorino and Pedro (Pete) Crawford, who would be a respected member of the Three Rivers community. By the late nineteenth century, other Hispanic families, including the Montoyas, Portillos and Lopezes, had settled in the area. Gretchen Heitzler described Pete Crawford:

> *Pete Crawford was our neighbor. He owned several acres right in the midst of the sixty thousand, and so far as I could find out, he'd lived there forever. His mother was a Spanish-American girl and his father a soldier…at Ft. Stanton…*
>
> *I have never know anyone like Pete Crawford. If he had been out of Lincoln or Otero County, I never heard of it. He could neither read nor write, nor could he speak English. He was in his fifties (I guess) when I became his neighbor. He wore a mustache, was rather short and stocky, and carried himself like a general. He rarely smiled, tended to his own affairs and asked favors of no one. Occasionally he rode a horse to Three Rivers to get mail and supplies when the store was open, but he never stopped at our house. For the first two years, the most recognition I received from Mr. Crawford was a tip of his hat.*

He lived somewhere near the up-the-river road in a small but immaculate adobe, and without knowing how to read, write, or speak English, he managed to hold onto his property until the end. With all the sharpies operating in that area, I guess that says something.[45]

Pete Crawford was still living on his ranch in the 1950s:

Pete Crawford had owned a section of ranch north of the church. When Tom [Ryan] *bought the ranch, he carved out the section for Pete for as long as he was alive. Pete would help with the branding. He came to New Mexico during the Civil War. All black. Very nice. Always friendly. No family. After he died, Forty Ryan lived on his section.*[46]

By the late 1880s and '90s, a few Anglos had also settled in the Three Rivers area; among the first were the Hytes. In these days of initial settlement, the amount of land owned by the settlers was limited only by economics and the availability of water. Stock was allowed to graze on the open range as long as the settler could control them. Ranchers with thousands of head of sheep and goats were said to have grazed the area from the low elevations of the basin to the slopes of the mountains.

The Bar W Ranch, or Carrizozo Cattle Company, was first owned by an unknown Hispanic family and then purchased by Thomas B. Catron and his brother-in-law, E.A. Walz. The Bar W claimed grazing rights from White

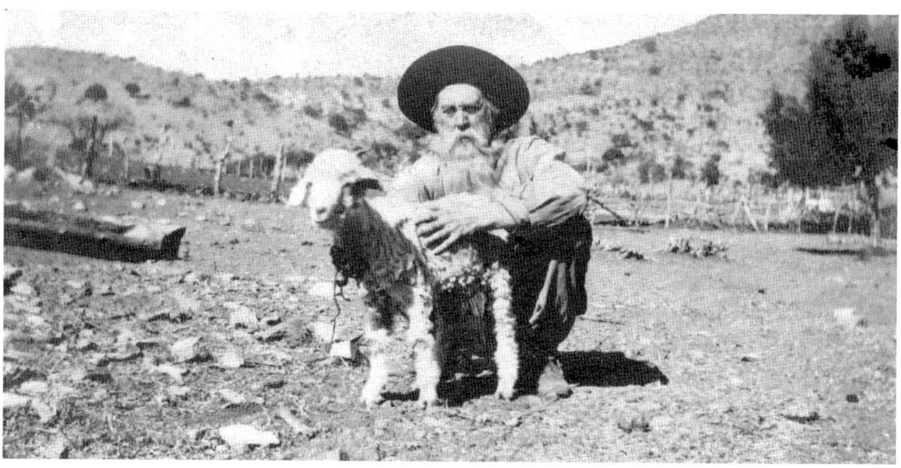

Unknown Three Rivers sheepherder, circa 1940. *Photo courtesy of Tularosa Basin Historical Society, Image P323.*

Oaks to the Texas border in the south and included the Three Rivers area. Catron sold a portion of his ranch to James A. Alcock in 1882 for $225,000.

Alcock ran his cattle herd both on his landholdings as well as on public land and watered them from six strong springs. He soon added more public lands to his operation, including twelve more springs. However, he was somewhat blocked in the Three Rivers area by sheepherder Dionisio Chavez. Chavez sold his water rights to Alcock for $3,888 but continued to use the area for his sheep, using secret and previously unknown springs. Things came to a head in June 1884, when seven hundred sheep were killed. Alcock and four other men were arrested and tried, but no sentence was ever handed down.[47]

During the first forty years of settlement, before grazing laws were passed and enforced, many small homesteads started in the Three Rivers area were almost always associated with water—tanks, ditches and fields. These homesteads ended with range control and "sole lease" rights taken up with the sale of most smallholdings into the single "ranching unit" of Albert Fall in 1906. An immigrant from Kentucky and Tennessee, Fall amassed his fortune through investments, legal services and "Colonel" Bill Greene's mining enterprises in Mexico.

Purchasing as many local ranches as possible, Fall consolidated his holdings to rival any others in the West. He next obtained grazing rights to local public land, which meant the end of family ranches. One result was that these small ranchers eventually became employees of Fall. The arrival of the railroad also brought jobs and economic prosperity to the basin. Engineering improvements to improve access to and use of water completed this period of change.

One family who lived on the eastern side of Three Rivers during the Depression was the Arthur Truax family, who raised Angora goats.

The mid- to late 1870s saw the entrance of a fascinating Irish rogue named Patrick Coghlan, who controlled Three Rivers until 1887. Thereafter, a series of lesser individuals came and went until Albert Bacon Fall arrived on the scene around 1906. Fall dominated Three Rivers until his economic and political downfall in the late 1920s because of his involvement in the national Teapot Dome Scandal. Three Rivers declined because of the Great Depression and a drought that all but forced abandonment of the area. The unlikely savior of the area came in the person of Thomas Fortune Ryan III, who bought the old Coghlan Ranch in the mid-1940s.

Patrick Coghlan

Patrick Coghlan was born in Clonakilty, County Cork, Ireland, on March 14, 1822. He immigrated to the United States in 1845 and enlisted in the U.S. Army. He ended his service in Texas in 1852 and farmed in Mason County for three years before moving to the town of Mason, where he kept a store and ran cattle. In 1862, he married Irish-born Anna A. Crosby, and they settled on a farm in Menard County.

In 1873, he moved west to the Hondo Valley in New Mexico (driving before him, according to one witness, a herd of cattle stolen from his own father-in-law). Coghlan next moved to La Luz, where he had an affair with the area's most famous madam, known only as Sadie. When Anna found out, she left him and was not heard from again.[48]

A controversial figure, he next moved to and began buying town lots in the village of Tularosa—so many that people began calling him the "King of Tularosa." Coghlan also established a general store on the plaza, a saloon and a wagon yard that provided him access to the gossip of all of Tularosa's comings and goings. Mrs. Coghlan is rumored to have donated a bell to the church. The current Tularosa Police Station sits on the site of Coghlan's house.[49]

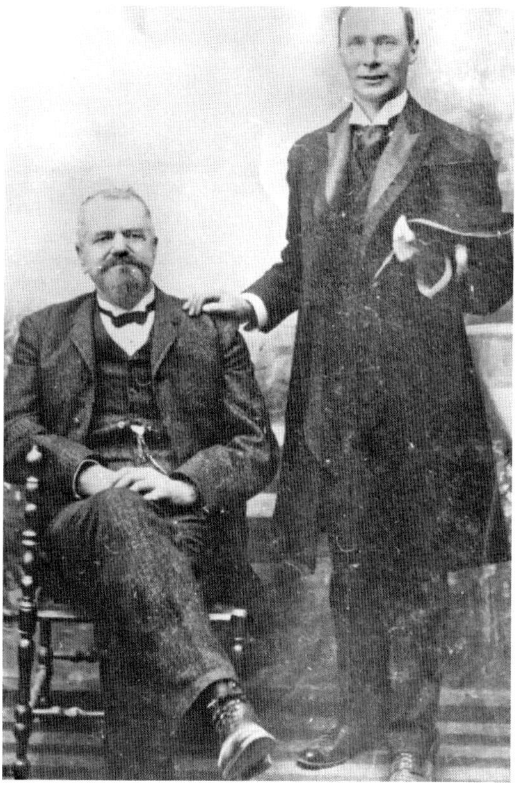

The King of Tularosa. Patrick Coghlan (left) and Lieutenant Norton (right), circa 1880s. *Photo courtesy of New Mexico State University Library, Archives and Special Collections, Herman Weisner Collection, Image C/1/5a.*

At the time, Tularosa was the hub of Tularosa Basin. Alamogordo and Carrizozo did not yet exist, and La Luz remained a small village of Hispanic immigrants, while White Oaks was just beginning to be settled after the discovery of gold in the northern end of the basin.

Coghlan, like many of the immigrants of the day, was always looking for ways to make a quick buck—even if, in his case, the means were questionable. Colorful and flamboyant, he was an astute businessman and quickly became the most prominent settler in the region, owning one thousand acres at Three Rivers, where he built a huge ranch house with three-feet-thick adobe walls. Coghlan was reported to have then declared that he had found his home.[50]

John Meadows described the land around Coghlan's home:

> *By the way, the land south of the old Coghlan residence was an arroyo started by that flood of 1881 which has been growing a little year by year ever since until now it is a terrible gash in the earth. Where the* [Albert B.] *Fall home is now, was a cienega or marsh at that time. The arroyo drained it and that spot is now dry ground. Also, the flood caused a stream to break forth near the mouth of Three Rivers Canyon, and which is where the Hatchet Ranch now gets its supply of water.*[51]

Once he had acquired his home place, Coghlan began to expand by acquiring Jose Chavez's grazing rights and purchasing Bar KL cattle. In addition to his house, located about five miles east of where the railroad is today, he built corrals and a barn. His place, an oasis in the desert, was the preferred stopping place for people traveling north through the area. His ranch grew from the I Bar X Ranch in the north to just three miles above Tularosa Creek in the south and from the boundary of today's Mescalero Reservation in the east to U.S. Highway 54 in the west.

The year 1877 found Coghlan a major taxpayer in Lincoln County and charged $107.35 on his property. He bid on a forage contract in July of that year, offering one hundred tons of bottomland hay for $18.00 a ton. A major economic player, he was also rumored to have received "loans" of government supplies from Mescalero agent Frederick C. Godfroy.

The next year, darker events involving Coghlan began to surface. On August 2, 1878, Antonio and Juliangero Sanchez, rumored to be Coghlan's hit men, killed James B. Reese in Tularosa. Things would get worse.

Victorio left the Mescalero Reservation in April 1879 and raided Coghlan's Three Rivers ranch. Ironically, despite all such raids, Coghlan's ranch prospered.

In April 1880, Coghlan won the contract to supply beef to the Mescalero Reservation at Fort Stanton and soon linked himself to rustlers like Billy the Kid, whose inroads into the herds of Panhandle ranchers had brought famed cattle detective Charlie Siringo and his group to New Mexico. On

February 18, 1881, Siringo found the hides of five LX steers at the Fort Stanton slaughterhouse owned by Coghlan and operated by former Lincoln County sheriff George Peppin. On August 16, the grand jury indicted Coghlan on eleven counts of "illegally purchasing cattle." He took a change of venue to Doña Ana County, where, in March 1882, he pleaded guilty to one count and paid a fine of $250; the other charges were dropped.

Siringo was not the only one who questioned Coghlan and his cattle purchases. John Meadows, an employee of Coghlan's at the Three Rivers ranch, became suspicious when he found some cattle bearing brands of well-known Texas ranches. He wrote:

> *In February* [sic, January 1881] *I had gone to work for Pat Coghlan and he had sent me word to stay put at Three Rivers. The first thing I done was to go around over the range and get acquainted with it. I went upon Indian River and found about forty-five head of cattle there with brands that were different than Coghlan's.*[52]

Meadows claims he informed George Nesmith of the stolen cattle he had found at Indian River and that Nesmith asked him the brands. Meadows told Nesmith, and Nesmith replied that Coghlan had bought them from Tom Cooper and Charlie Bowdre. Meadows next went to Pat Coghlan and confronted him about the stolen cattle. Coghlan claimed that it was all right and to go ahead and include those cattle with the Fort Stanton contract and he would back him up.[53]

About the first of February, Coghlan sent word for Meadows to meet him at Tularosa, which he did. On the return to Three Rivers, Meadows met Charles Siringo going from Three Rivers (where he had spent the night) to Tularosa. Siringo informed Meadows he was working for the Canadian Cattlemen's Association looking for stolen cattle with the same brands Meadows had discovered the previous month. Siringo told Meadows not to say anything and continued on to Tularosa.

Siringo went into Tularosa and, after locating Coghlan, asked about the cattle. Coghlan denied any knowledge of such cattle, and Siringo returned to Three Rivers.

The next day, Siringo rode out, found the stolen cattle and went to White Oaks to consult with Jim East, who was also with the group looking for stolen cattle. East sent Siringo back to Tularosa by way of Fort Stanton, where he found more hides of stolen cattle. Traveling on to Tularosa, Siringo confronted Coghlan.

Caught red-handed, Coghlan agreed not to sell these beeves but to hold them until the next spring, when Siringo could come and take the cattle in question back to Texas. On his way out, Siringo met with Meadows, who asked him to talk to George Nesmith, a likely star witness for him.

Shortly afterward, Meadows went to Tularosa to tell Coghlan that four hundred head of Coghlan's cattle had been stolen and driven to Hembrillo Canyon. Coghlan rounded up some cowboys, and Siringo spent the night at Three Rivers talking to Mr. and Mrs. Nesmith.

Later that spring, Coghlan approached Meadows, asking him to take the cattle to Fort Stanton and put them on his account (in violation of Coghlan's agreement with Siringo). Meadows refused to take the cattle to Fort Stanton. Coghlan fired Meadows on the spot, and Meadows left the ranch.[54]

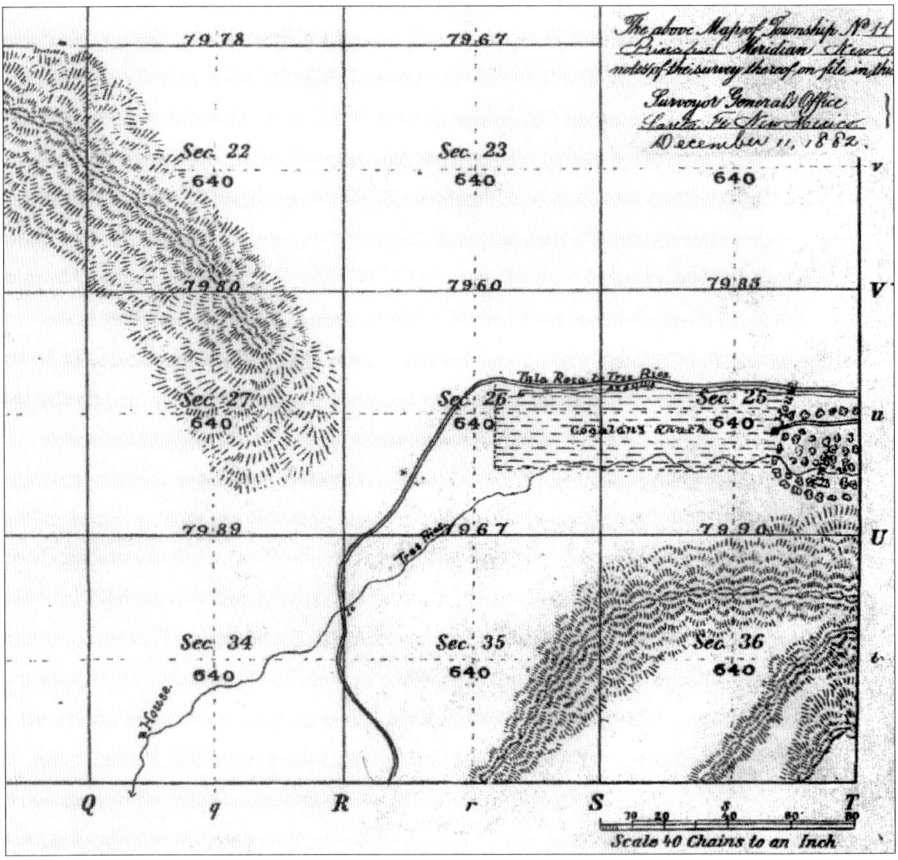

An 1882 map of the Three Rivers area showing Pat Coghlan's ranch. *Surveyor General of New Mexico, Map of Township No. 11, December 11, 1882.*

Meadows concluded: "About March or April, Pat Coghlan and I had a falling out, and he discharged me and paid me off. The last thing I said to him was 'them LX, LITS and LS cattle will be bellowing around your bed-post the first thing you know.'"[55]

The preceding September, Coghlan employee George Nesmith (Clifford calls them "Nesbitt"); his wife, Lucy; and their adopted four-year-old daughter had been found murdered. It was not until March 1885 that two suspects, Ruperto Lara and Maximo Apodaca, were arrested. Lara confessed that Coghlan had offered him $1,000, a wagon and a pair of horses to kill the Nesmiths. Coghlan was arrested for complicity in the murders, but when Apodaca contested Lara's statement saying no offer of money had been made and Lara was unable to identify Coghlan in a lineup of twenty-five men, Coghlan was released.

By April 16, 1886, Coghlan was in financial trouble. He had executed a mortgage deed to Numa Reymond and Martin Lohman for $15,000, seemingly unaware the interest rates he was paying could wipe him out. This was followed by another promissory note to Reymond for $26,795.48 in 1892 at 12 percent interest. By 1897, the note was worth $32,000. W.W. Cox bought the note and sold a third each to Oliver Lee and Fitzgerald Moore. Wipe him out they did; on January 16, 1906, he signed a warranty deed to Albert B. Fall, who had bought up his notes, leaving Coghlan in straitened circumstances.

His wife (some said Pat had divorced his first wife, Anna, and this was her sister) died in 1903; Coghlan himself, now frail and palsied, died on January 27, 1911, and was buried as a forgotten man in El Paso.

Mrs. Jim Baird wrote of him:

> *He was a powerful man physically, an all-around athlete of his time, and had a lively disposition. He never turned a deaf ear to the cry of the poor; always a great lover of children; never too busy to talk to them in their sports. Peace to his ashes. May the sod rest lightly on his breast.*[56]

BILLY THE KID, CHARLES SIRINGO AND GEORGE NESMITH

Every region of old Lincoln County has been touched by William H. Bonney, alias Billy the Kid, and Three Rivers is no exception.

Local legend has it that Billy the Kid and Coghlan were friends and "business associates" and that about five miles east of the railroad station,

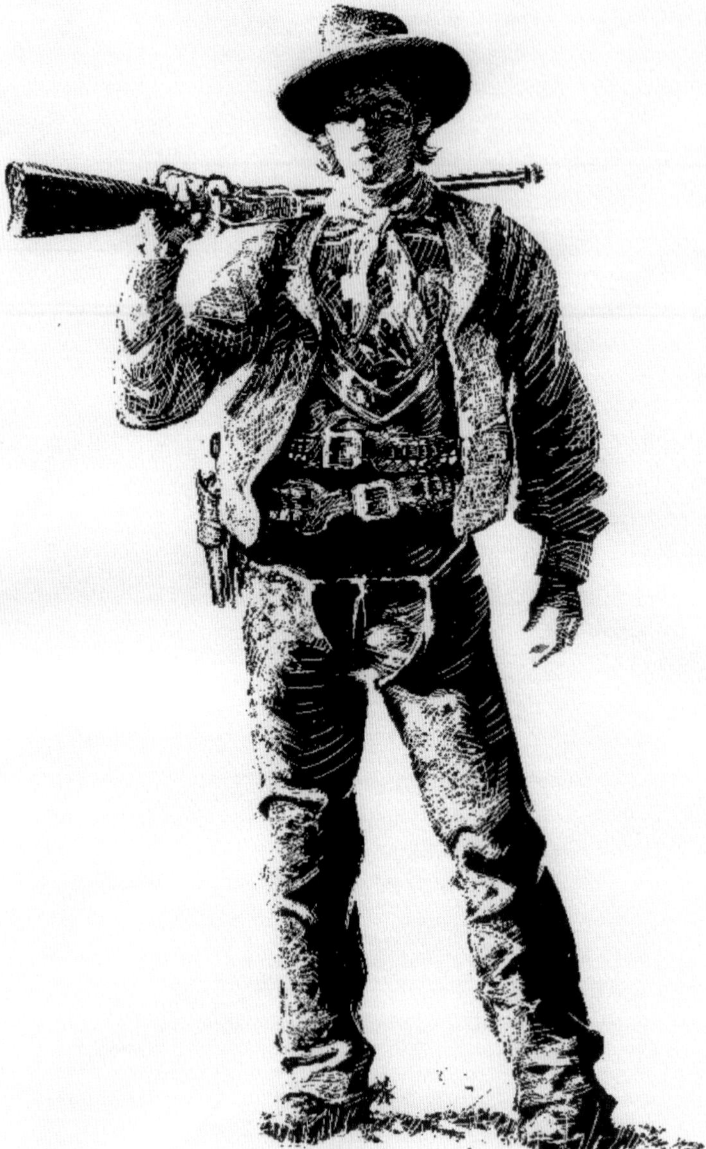

William Bonney, alias Billy the Kid, cattle rustler for Patrick Coghlan. *Drawing courtesy of Bob Boze Bell.*

there was a small adobe house where Billy the Kid is rumored to have stayed when he brought stolen cattle to Pat and hid rustled stock on Coughlan's place. Bonney reportedly would steal cattle in Texas, as well as from John Chisum's

Pecos South Spring ranch, and then drive them to Three Rivers, where Coughlan would butcher them or sell them beef-on-the-hoof to the army at Fort Stanton for use by the fort or the Mescaleros at nearby reservations.

One rancher whose stock went missing was John Chisum, whose ranch was on the Pecos River south of present-day Roswell. At one time, Billy the Kid was also friendly with John Chisum and his cowboys (until "Jinglebob" cattle were found on Coghlan's Three Rivers ranch. These cattle were either butchered on Coghlan's ranch or sold on the hoof).

After Coghlan's illegal activities were reported to Texas Panhandle cattlemen, they contracted Frank Stewart to discover what was happening to their missing cattle. Stewart soon uncovered the connection between the Kid's rustling and Coghlan. Stewart got to within forty miles of Three Rivers when he turned back, confessing he had "too few men," but in fact was rumored to have turned around when Coghlan was said to have told him that Stewart would have to recover the cattle with hot lead.[57]

Under the leadership of William C. "Outlaw Bill" Monroe, the Texas ranchers next turned to Charles Siringo to put an end to their loss of cattle. After Monroe supplied Siringo and his cowboys a chuck wagon and four mules, they went to New Mexico in search of the stolen Texas herds. Moore's orders to Siringo were to stay in New Mexico until he either recovered the cattle or broke the LX Ranch.

Siringo was backed by five men: James East, Lee Hall, Lon Chambers, Cal Polk and Frank Clifford, also know as "Big Foot Wallace." Moore instructed Siringo to stay until they got the job done and even gave Siringo extra funds for replacement horses and feed. In February 1881, Siringo and Tom Emory rode first to Fort Stanton, where they found freshly skinned hides bearing the LX brand at Coghlan's butcher shop. From there, the men went to Three Rivers to confront Pat Coghlan. They took several witnesses along who could testify that the beeves were recently sold to the army by Pat Coghlan.[58]

Siringo eventually caught up with Coghlan at Las Cruces, telling Coghlan he came to get the cattle Coghlan had bought from Billy the Kid. Coghlan responded that Siringo would not get them and claimed he had a crowd at White Oaks to take the cattle by force if necessary.[59]

The beginning of Coghlan's downfall came in the form of George Nesmith, a recent settler who had come to New Mexico as a sergeant of Company A, Fifth California Infantry in the California Column, during the Civil War. Born in Ohio about 1843, Nesmith was discharged from the army at Mesilla on November 30, 1864. He married Lucy Newcomb of El Paso four years later and first settled at Blazer's Mill, where he and partners Dr. Blazer and George H. Abbott purchased a sawmill known as La Maquina.

Blazer eventually bought Nesmith out in 1876, and Nesmith and his wife took up farming at Three Rivers. Coghlan repeatedly offered to buy Nesmith out, and after repeated refusals, Coghlan made Nesmith the general caretaker of his Three Rivers ranch. Made of a better moral fiber, the Nesmiths had a hard time accepting the illegal activities happening with the cattle.

Siringo finally talked Coghlan into accepting a deal in which he would confess to his illegal activities but would serve no jail time. Siringo would be allowed to round up the Texas cattle and drive them back to their rightful owners, but this would take time (according to Coghlan because the cattle were scattered throughout Coghlan's spread). Though it was obviously a stalling tactic, both sides agreed, and Siringo spent the night at the Three Rivers Ranch, where he met the Nesmiths.[60]

Departing the next morning for White Oaks, Siringo was accompanied by a Mexican guide. On the way to White Oaks, Siringo was ambushed (no doubt by Coghlan's men) and would likely have been killed if he had not veered off the trail. In the meantime, Coghlan had driven all remaining LX cattle to Fort Stanton to sell them. Observing this, Nesmith sent a note to Siringo telling him about the cattle being taken to Fort Stanton and offered to take responsibility for the move.[61]

Siringo notified Moore to prosecute and immediately rode with "Big Foot" Wallace to Fort Stanton, where they found fresh LX hides hanging on a fence. Traveling quickly to Three Rivers and arriving after midnight, Siringo and Wallace discovered eight head of LX cattle, all that remained of the stolen herd. The eight steers were driven to White Oaks and held as evidence. Combined with Nesmith's testimony, the evidence would be overwhelming. Siringo then returned to the LX Ranch via Fort Sumner and Portales Springs, arriving on June 22, 1881.[62]

Lincoln County sheriff John W. Poe traveled to Three Rivers, where he put Coghlan under arrest. (Poe was also on retainer to Moore and the Canadian River Cattle Association.) Coghlan reportedly offered Poe a substantial bribe, which Poe refused. Poe summoned Siringo and Chambers to testify at Coghlan's trial. Arriving in Lincoln just prior to the November 7 trial, Siringo was informed that Coghlan had received a change of venue to Mesilla because the court feared enemies in Lincoln County, and Poe instructed Siringo to appear at the trial on the first Monday in April 1882.

The *Santa Fe New Mexican* provided a good summary of the situation, quoting John Poe:

> *Cattle were stolen from the Pan-handle by Billy the Kid, Charley Bowdry* [sic], *and others. They were driven to White Oaks and turned over to one Tom Cooper, a noted thief who was in the country at that time. By Cooper they were driven to Coghlan, of Tularosa, who bought them from him, paying $12.00 per head for four and five year old beef steers…Beef steers at the time were $25 to $27 per head. At the August* [1881] *term of the court, in Lincoln County, the Grand Jury found seven indictments against Coghlan for buying, receiving, concealing, and selling stolen cattle, the property of D.T. Beals, of the Panhandle. Coghlan butchered most of the cattle at Fort Stanton, and turned them in on his Government beef contracts. Some of the cattle had been killed by him after they had been claimed by their owners, and after the latter had notified Coghlan not to kill any more of them.*[63]

The *Daily New Mexican* continued:

> *At the November* [1881] *term of the court in Lincoln County Coghlan took a change of venue to Dona Ana with his cases. This was done merely to keep the trial off with the hope that some of the witnesses for the prosecution might leave the country. At the March* [1882] *term of the court in Dona Ana County Mr. Coghlan was not ready for trial, and pretended that he could not get his witnesses—after seven months he could not get his witnesses. At the same time he met and was in company with one of them in Santa Fe about a month before court, and the other one he wanted was known to have been living in El Paso for some time before the court convened in Mesilla, and within Coghlan's easy reach, if he had wanted him. Coghlan failed to get a continuance. His attorneys tried to quash the indictment, but failed. Finally one of the Coghlan cases was set for trial, one in which the proof was positive against him, but it seemed that something always came in the way when the time came round for trial. Coghlan at last proposed to plead guilty in one of the cases—the one in which the penalty was the least—provided the others were thrown out of course. Parties representing the owners of the cattle losing confidence in the prosecuting attorney consented, and Coghlan entered the plea of guilty and was fined $150. The prosecuting attorney entered a nolle prosequi in all the other cases.*[64]

Poe, Siringo and Pat Garrett testified against Coghlan when the trial began in April 1882.[65] Forced to testify against neighbor and employer, the

Nesmiths were scheduled to testify next. Mrs. Nesmith summed it up with precision when she said, "I am afraid to go by the White Sands. So many terrible things have happened there. It is so lonely there. I just feel terrible about taking this trip."[66] The Nesmiths never arrived at the courtroom.[67]

On August 17, 1882, the Nesmiths and their adopted daughter, Lucy, disappeared as they passed through the White Sands on their way to Mesilla to testify in Coghlan's trial. Two weeks later, prospectors spotted the couple's wagon with badly decomposed bodies, identified by George's watch and Mrs. Nesmith's trunk. Missing was Nesmith's overcoat made by Las Cruces seamstress Mrs. Tucker. Tucker had run out of lining material when she made the coat so she substituted dress material, thereby making the coat easy to identify.

John Meadows said the Nesmiths and their four-year-old daughter, Lucy, left Blazer's Mill in a lumber wagon on August 16 or 17 on their way to Las Cruces. About midday, they ate lunch at the Coghlan Well on the south end of the White Sands, where they picked up two Mexicans who were afoot and traveling the same direction. Toward the end of the day near Chalk Hill, Nesmith told Maximo Apodaca (who was by then driving the wagon) to turn off the road so they could find a place to camp for the night. Ruperto Lara, who was walking behind the wagon, then put a pistol to Nesmith's head and killed him. He then shot Mrs. Nesmith in the same manner.

The two Mexicans had driven the wagon parallel to the main road for two and a half miles when Lara stopped the wagon and told Apodaca he had to kill the baby since he had killed the parents. Apodaca grabbed the child by the feet and bashed her head on the wagon wheel. Lara and Apodaca then got on the two horses that had been pulling the wagon and rode into Mexico.

As Tom O'Connor and Sam Barlin were traveling across the Tularosa Basin eighteen miles north of San Augustine on September 6, 1882, near San Nicolas Spring, they saw buzzards gathered around an abandoned wagon. When they got close, they found blood splattered over a wide area and lifeless forms. The two men hastened to Shedd's Ranch, where they reported what they had seen. The next morning, a mounted party went back to the site, where they found the bodies of a man, woman and young girl. Robbery did not appear to be the motive, as there was still a trunk in the wagon.

It was estimated the victims had been dead two weeks. Thoughts were that this was the Nesmith family, who had disappeared en route to testifying against Patrick Coghlan, or possibly John Gray. Speculation ended when Gray, a resident of Tularosa, showed up. The bodies were then identified as the Nesmith family, and Gray, Wesley Fields, H.C. Brown and another man from Tularosa buried the little family at Blazer's Mill next to another Nesmith child who had died previously.[68]

The *Rio Grande Republican* described events this way:

> *Last Wednesday, as Tom O'Connor and Sam Barlin were cutting across the unfrequented country which lies between St. Nicholas Spring and the Jarillas, they saw at some distance from them an abandoned wagon. On closer approach, they saw that it was lined with buzzards, and a wolf or two sneaked away on being discovered. Soon they saw the blood which had oozed from the wagon, and spread itself over the axles and wheels, and collected on pools on the ground. But more overpowering than all was the horrible odor which filled the air for a mile off. After this hasty survey, and catching a glimpse of the outline of some still figures in the body of the wagon, they hurried on to San Augustine with their ghastly tidings.*
>
> *Next morning a party left Shedd's ranch for the horrible place, which is about eighteen miles from San Augustine on the Tularosa road; but the wagon is not visible from the road, the distance from it being too great. They found that the tires were rusty from disuse, and the horses gone though the harness was left entire, except the bridles, by which, doubtless the horses had been led away. In the wagon were some papers and an account book belonging to George Nesmith, of Three Rivers—a person well known in Las Cruces—also, a trunk, unrifled, and a silver watch.*
>
> *There were three corpses in the wagon. One was that of a man, who had been shot in the forehead, another that of a woman who had been shot in the mouth, and the third, that of a little girl, about eight years old, the means of whose death was not visible. The bodies were all found decently covered by blankets, but were so decomposed as to be unrecognizable. They were all carefully buried, and had been dead probably two weeks…*
>
> *The body was not that of Mr. Nesmith, it was too short and not stout enough. Yet Nesmith is missing, and was obviously in or near the wagon at the time of the murder. He had a wife and an adopted little girl, but this one was said to be too large for the child. The body of the man just might be that of his partner or assistant, Gray, as the appearance would justify such an assumption. But why was Gray murdered and where was Nesmith?*
>
> *The deed was not of Indians or rustlers, evidently, as no robbery was committed. Indians would never have covered up the body so carefully with blankets, and we have never yet heard of rustlers who were base and cowardly as to kill a little girl.*

> *The mystery is not impenetrable, and may soon be solved. When Nesmith is found, and the wagon, trunk and watch, and the clothing of the victims, are identified by parties from Three Rivers, the whole matter may be cleared up. But that a terrible crime has been committed is too evident to be doubted for a moment.*[69]

A week later, the paper carried an even more vivid account of the events, even taking potshots at Sheriff Pat Garrett:

> *Some weeks since, at a date which we have not precisely ascertained, George Nesmith left Tularosa with his wife and their adopted child, a little girl, in his wagon, for Las Cruces. The party never reached here; and the wagon has been identified as his. The clothing on the woman was that of Mrs. Nesmith, and a trunk and its contents which were on the wagon were also known to have been hers. An account book and some papers belonging to Nesmith were found under the seat; and if the body of the man had proved to be that of Nesmith, the inference would have been clear that the whole party had been murdered either out of revenge or to obtain some private end. Robbery was out of the question. There was little to take, and that little was not touched. Nor has even the wildest fancy laid it to the charge of the Indians, as there was no trace whatsoever of their presence.*
>
> *But is the body that of Geo. Nesmith? We have personally spoken to three of the parties who went out to identify and bury the bodies, and they are all decidedly of the opinion that it is not; but we must remember that death and corruption strangely alter the features and forms of persons, and if this is not Nesmith's body, then whose is it?...*
>
> *Many rumors are flying about in connection with this dark deed. One was that Nesmith was seen in El Paso only a few days since; but Mr. Shedd has just come up from there, and tho' he made strict enquiries* [sic], *he could not find anyone who had met him. Another was that a negro and a Mexican were seen about the supposed time of the murder, leading by the bridle a horse resembling Nesmith's, with the blinders cut off, and it will be remembered that the blinders of Nesmith's team had been cut off, and were found near the harness; but the clue was not traced up, and the parties have disappeared.*
>
> *The mystery remains just as it did last week. If this is Nesmith's body, why was he murdered? And if it is not, as the three witnesses assert, then whose body is it, and what brought it there?*
>
> *Incredible as it may seem, none of the so-called officers of justice either in Lincoln or Dona Ana counties have taken the slightest interest in the*

affair, or taken one step to apprehend the criminals. What is the famous Pat Garrett about? The bodies ought assuredly to be disinterred, their identity placed beyond question, and a coroner's inquest held over them. The case we learn is before the grand jury, and we took occasion to pump one of the jurors; but he either knew or would reveal nothing.[70]

Governor A.L. Sheldon offered a $500 reward, and outraged citizens of Lincoln and Dona Ana Counties soon set up a reward for the arrest and conviction of the murderer or murderers. The amount privately offered eventually grew to more than $580, and strangely enough, "Mr. P. Coghlan writes that he wishes to add his name to the list of subscribers to the Nesmith fund; that he will give as much, and is just as anxious for the apprehension of the murderer, as any one of his neighbors."[71]

Before long, word of the murders spread, and it was reported that a Mexican had been seen wearing the coat. That individual crossed the Rio Grande one step ahead of the law and remained there for over four years. Eventually, Maximo Apodaca and Rupert Lara crossed back into the United States and were arrested, tried and found guilty of murder.[72]

A Mrs. Tucker of Tularosa had made George Nesmith a custom overcoat and had used dress material as a lining. It was believed that Nesmith was wearing the coat at the time of the murder, and the coat was missing. Milt Reed, a butcher from Las Cruces, went to Hatch to buy some cattle when he saw the unusual coat hanging in a hut. Reed went to Deputy Sheriff James Lloyd and told him what he had found. Lloyd then went to the owner of the hut and asked about the coat. The owner said it belonged to a man named Apodaca. When confronted by Lloyd, Apodaca confessed immediately. He identified Lara, who was then living in Juarez, as his accomplice.

Lloyd and John Walters of Bent went to Juarez, where they found Lara making adobe bricks. After convincing Lara they wanted to buy horses, he purchased horses and took them to El Paso, where the pair was promptly arrested and brought before a grand jury. Lara refused to make a statement, but Apodaca confessed to the murder.

Apodaca testified that the two men had been near Tularosa stealing cattle, with Lara riding a horse and Apodaca on foot, when they came upon the Nesmiths near White Water. The Nesmiths fed the two men and gave Apodaca a ride in their wagon. About halfway to San Augustine, on a prearranged signal, Lara killed the couple, and Apodaca killed the child. The pair then drove the wagon a mile or so off the main road and took Nesmith's black overcoat, Mrs. Nesmith's black shawl and some blankets and mounted the horses, taking them to their home across the border to Santa Barbara, where Lara gave the overcoat to his father.[73]

The *Rio Grande Republican* followed up on its earlier stories with the following account:

> *Not long ago James Lloyd, who was instrumental in the discovery of the murderers, making the arrests, and to whom is due the full credit of unraveling the mystery, found a coat that was known to be the property of Nesmith, and which he had in his possession when he met his death. With this clue, with considerable skill as a detective, he traced the case until he found that the coat had been bought from a man who lives in Santa Barbara, this county, by Felipe Telles, of the same place.*
>
> *This man, whose name we could not learn, had a son-in-law, Ruperto Lara, who together with one Maximo Apodaca, was known to be in the neighborhood at the time the murder was committed. The man Lara was placed under suspicion, but as it was learned that he was across from El Paso, in Mexico, a scheme was devised to get him on this side of the river, which was successfully accomplished last Saturday.*
>
> *Maximo Apodaca was also placed under arrest together with Felipe Telles, who brought the coat, and Tuesday they were brought before the Grand Jury where Apodaca made a full confession. He says they talked about killing Nesmith for his team before they left Tularosa, but the scheme was not consummated before they reached the neighborhood of the place where the bodies were found. Lara first shot the man and woman with a pistol and then, as Apodaca stated, to show he was as brave as Lara, he ended the life of the little girl with a ball from his rifle. All of this happened on the main road and after the killing they drove the team about two miles to a point that was out of sight and went through the trunk taking out some silverware…*
>
> *From the spoils obtained from this bloody deed that rivals anything published in fiction, Apodaca's share was a blanket, a quilt, a pair of pants and coat. The blanket is in the possession of the authorities. The remainder of the good he says were either lost or worn out. Lara took the coat and silverware.*
>
> *The murders were committed shortly after dark and then they got on the horses and rode about 50 miles to the San Diego crossing on the Rio Grande, arriving there the next morning. Here they parted, Lara offering Apodaca one of the horses which he refused to take. Lara then left, riding one horse and leading the other.*[74]

While Apodaca pleaded guilty, Lara steadfastly maintained his innocence. The territory was represented by District Attorney Wade and assisted by Colonel Albert J. Fountain, Judge Newcomb and William Rynerson. Attorneys E.B. Beer and Aikman Welch represented the defendants. Jury selection took almost two days. Apodaca was the first witness to testify for the territory. He described the murders in detail and testified, "I killed that child." Mrs. Tucker easily identified the overcoat, and the jury had little difficulty finding Lara guilty. Attorneys Beer and Welch offered no defense. The jury deliberated for five minutes before returning a verdict of guilty of murder in the first degree, and the pair were sentenced to be hanged by the neck until dead on April 30, 1885. Colonel Fountain then commuted Apodaca's punishment to life in prison due to his truthful testimony. The judge stated he would recommend it to the governor. [75]

Lara then made a full confession. Present at the trial was court interpreter and newspaper reporter George Butschofsky, who recorded Lara's confession:

> *I, Ruperto Lara, am a prisoner in the jail at Las Cruces, under sentence of death for the murder of George Nesmith and his family. My time is very short, and I've not long to live.*
>
> *Before I die I want to tell all about the murder of Nesmith and his family and how it was that I was induced to commit that crime. I thought I'd had some friends who'd help me in this trouble as they promised, but as it appears they have abandoned me to my faith, it is right that I should now speak and tell the truth.*

Lara stated that a man named Coghlan who lived in Tularosa "got me in this trouble" and added:

> *There is a man who lives in Tularosa who I had a right to look to for assistance; he should have been my friend for it is him who got me into this trouble; his name is Pat Coghlan, and he keeps a store in Tularosa.*
>
> *A short time before this thing happened, I was at Coghlan's store in Tularosa. There was present a man whose name I don't know, an American about the size of Mr. Fountain with a reddish or florid complexion and reddish hair and beard and mustache, Coghlan and this man talked about two hours while I was there, I bought some provisions and started off, when I was getting on my horse, Coghlan came out of the store and said he wanted to talk to me. He asked if I knew Geo. Nesmith, I said, no. He said Nesmith lived at Three Rivers on a ranch and was trying to jump a ranch*

> *that he, Coghlan, had at Three Rivers. He said if I would kill Nesmith he would pay me for it. I told him I could not do it...Then we had some more talk about what he wanted me to do and said he would give me $1,000 to kill Nesmith. He offered me a wagon and a pair of horses which he said were worth $300.*[76]

Coghlan asked Lara if he knew Nesmith, to which he replied he did not but Coghlan had told Lara that Nesmith lived on a ranch at Three Rivers and was trying to jump Coghlan's land. The conversation continued, and Lara eventually agreed to murder Nesmith in the presence of another man believed to have been Perry Kearney for $1,000, Nesmith's wagon and horses and a pick of the store's saddlebags.

Lara was told to go to the house of a black carpenter named Pompey at Three Rivers for instructions. When told to commit the murder, he was only given some money—the rest would be forthcoming after the murder. When Lara went to Coghlan to collect, Coghlan refused to pay, saying he needed proof of the murder.[77]

Lara was hanged on April 29, 1885, before an estimated 1,200 people, but Apodaca was given a life sentence because it was believed he had been forced at gunpoint to kill Nesmith's adopted daughter. Apodaca's sentence was commuted to imprisonment for life by Governor A.L. Sheldon; however, Apodaca committed suicide by jumping to his death from the fourth floor of the state prison from a height of sixty feet on November 4, 1885.[78]

Once Lara and Apodaca were punished, attention next turned to Coghlan's role in the murders. Coghlan initially had eight charges filed against him, but after some illegal activities, all charges were dismissed except that of buying stolen cattle. In the end, Coghlan pleaded guilty and paid a fine of $150. The day after Coghlan pleaded guilty, Albert J. Fountain filed a $10,000.00 lawsuit against Coghlan on behalf of the Panhandle ranchers, eventually winning $257.79 in one judgment and $120.80 in the other.

The *Rio Grande Republican* reported the outcome:

> *On the first day of last week, tho' we have not had space to report them before, as they were crowded out by the more important murder trials, the various cases of the* Territory vs. Patrick Coghlan *for purchasing cattle without receiving a bill of sale, &c., were taken up and disposed of by the court. The defendant was fined $150 in one case, and the remainder of the cases were dismissed, as this was the first time such a charge had ever been brought into the court. In imposing the penalty, the Judge remarked that it*

> *was an offense which nearly all, if not all, cattlemen in the district were guilty of, and advised that the attention of this class of our citizens be called to the fact of the existence of such a law on our statute books, as at present it was very little known and totally disregarded throughout our Territory.*[79]

The only problem with the newspaper's analysis is that Coghlan pleaded guilty to this single charge in order to avoid trial on several others.

With rustling charges behind him, Coghlan thought he was free of troubles. Lara and Apodaca were unable to pick Coghlan out of a lineup, and he escaped judgment in the Nesmiths' case. But his fortune, once estimated at over $100,000, was depleted. His predicament was exacerbated in that he could no longer rustle cattle since the Three Rivers country was seeing an influx of settlers—175 in 1885—which also brought law and order.[80]

Coghlan continued to travel, often leaving a minimum crew at the ranch, until he ran out of money. Desperate, he finally mortgaged heavily against the ranch with Sheriff Numa Reymond and Martin Lohman of Las Cruces. The initial loan was for $15,000.00, and in 1892, Coghlan borrowed another $26,795.48 at an interest rate of 12 percent. When the note was sold to W.W. Cox in 1887, it was valued at $32,000.00. Cox quickly divided the note into thirds, selling parts to Oliver Lee and Fitzgerald Moore.

A month later saw foreclosure, and Cox, Lee and Moore paid $22,500.00 for 1,025 head of cattle and $500.00 for 96 head of horses. As agent for the sale, Pat Garrett received $1,236.95. Coghlan went from a larger-than-life rancher to a man broken in both health and wealth.[81]

In 1903, Coghlan's wife, Ann, died, and in 1906, he signed a warranty deed to Albert B. Fall, who had bought the original deed from Numa Reymond. Although Coghlan pressed Fall to repay the remaining $5,000 equity, Fall got a compromise of $1,500. Fall next turned to his friends Cox, Lee and Moore and paid them interest for the next eight years.

Coghlan died on January 22, 1911, in Tularosa. His estate had dwindled to ten beds (from his old Tularosa hotel), his pistol, some books and several acres of land valued at $4,300.00. Mrs. E.B. Taylor claimed Coghlan owed her $1,382.20 and secured the estate, valued at $319.20 after all bills were paid. John P. Meadows purchased the Tularosa property. Coghlan's remains were taken to El Paso and buried in the Concordia Cemetery.[82]

SUSAN MCSWEEN BARBER—THE CATTLE QUEEN OF NEW MEXICO

Born on December 30, 1845, at Tyrone Township, Pennsylvania, Susan Hummer McSween grew up near Gettysburg and came to Lincoln with her husband, Alexander McSween, in March 1875. The McSweens immediately became thoroughly involved in local politics and the Lincoln County War as partisans on the side of John H. Tunstall. Alex lost his life during the final day of the "Five Day Battle" on July 19, 1878. Susan hung on in Lincoln and was an active participant in the aftermath of that bloodshed, including bringing charges against Lieutenant Colonel Augustus Dudley, which led to a formal court of inquiry into his conduct by the army. Dudley was eventually cleared of those charges, and Mrs. McSween continued her crusade against her husband's killers. Two years after her husband's death, she was still living in Lincoln, managing a 160-acre farm and raising a variety of domestic animals.

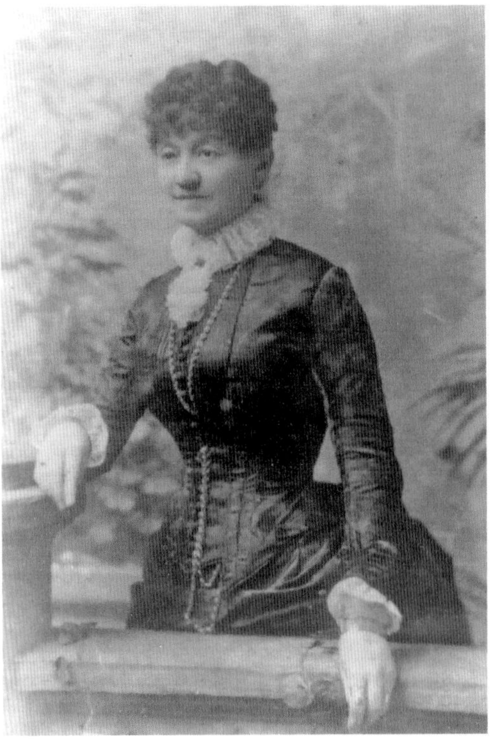

Cattle Queen of New Mexico Susan McSween Barber. *Photo courtesy of Lincoln County Historical Society, Image lchscol776.*

Susan McSween later, in 1880, married George Barber, a surveyor in Lincoln. Upon arriving in Lincoln, he studied law and was admitted to the New Mexico Bar in October 1882.

By January 1883, George Barber had patented four hundred acres northeast of Coghlan's property at Three Rivers under the Desert Land Act. Naming the ranch "SLS," Susan built a rock house, which became a local landmark. Among her first acts on the couple's claim was to construct a dam across Three Rivers and a half-mile ditch to bring water to her property. About this time, George Barber decided to move first to Lincoln and then to White Oaks and Carrizozo

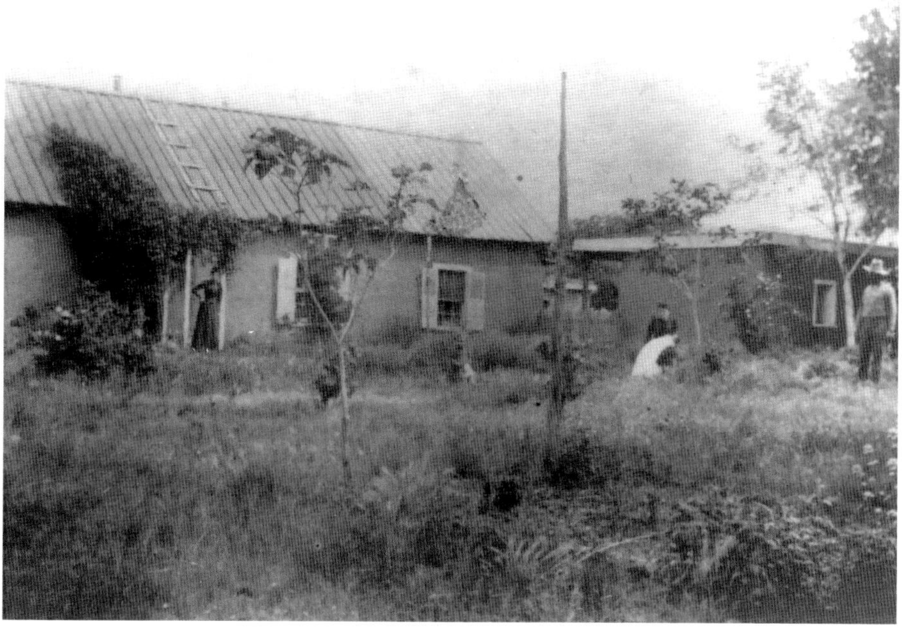

The Susan McSween Barber ranch house, circa 1880. *Photo courtesy of Lincoln County Historical Society Image lchs747.*

so he could return to practicing law and "capitalize on their resources." He never really became involved in the Three Rivers operation.[83]

The source of Mrs. Barber's cattle is vague. Some claim the cattle came from money paid to the estate of Alexander McSween, but most historians agree that John Chisum gave her cattle for a "starter herd." That herd was driven from Chisum's ranch on the Pecos to Nogal and then to Barber's Three Rivers ranch.[84]

By 1887, Susan had enlisted the aid of two partners from Milwaukee and was operating the ranch as its manager. Susan was on her way to becoming one of the fabled women in frontier New Mexico. By 1888, the ranch had expanded to 1,158 acres.

As manager, Susan ran every facet of the ranch. There are also some theories that she was assisted by a black foreman named earlier in this narrative as Pompey. She planned and supervised use of the land, hired and supervised the ranch hands and planted and harvested fields of vegetables, grain, berries and fruit trees. Mrs. Barber is said to have had over five thousand head of cattle, earning her the nickname the "Cattle Queen of New Mexico."[85]

Yet happiness eluded her. George Barber had sold his interest in the Three Rivers Land and Cattle Company by 1889, and Susan filed for divorce in September 1891, claiming that Barber had failed to support her during their marriage and had abandoned her. Barber next married twenty-two-year-old Eugenia Roberts less than a year later.[86]

Susan continually improved her ranch, often working side-by-side with her cowboys while still wearing skirts. She fought off attempts by Pat Coghlan to take over her place and also confronted her neighbor to the north, Lin Branum, owner of the I Bar X Ranch. When it appeared that Branum was intruding on her land, Barber sent her foreman, Pompey, to talk to Branum. When gunfire ensued, Pompey was wounded, and Branum ran for Oklahoma. Cooler heads prevailed, and good relations between the two soon-to-be ranch titans lasted for the remainder of Barber's time at Three Rivers.

J. Denton Simms, one of Mrs. Barber's Three Rivers neighbors who had migrated from Texas, observed,

> *One of our more interesting neighbors was Mrs. Susan Barber, the elderly widow of Alexander McSween…*
>
> *Mrs. Barber as she was now called because of a subsequent marriage, was again a widow and lived near us in a historic landmark known locally as "The Rock House." She was thought to be very wealthy and enjoyed being called the "Cattle Queen of New Mexico." Wealthy or not, she still owned and wore an impressive display of diamonds and visited around the community in a fine buggy driven by a man she called Pompey. Mother recalled that when Mrs. Barber came to call on us she was dressed in taffeta, wearing a wide hat decorated with ostrich plumes. Pompey was as wide as he was long, Mother says in her memoirs, and Mrs. Barber told her that when he wore out a pair of overalls he would not take them off but just put a new pair over the old. Sometimes he would have four or five pairs of pants on at one time.*
>
> *Mrs. Barber loved to go to the dances that were held a various ranches. My brother Donald, who was forced to dance with her on one of these occasions, complained about how stiff her legs were…*
>
> *When A.B. Fall came into the country and began to take over all the land he could get, Mrs. Barber refused to sell to him. She did sell to a neighbor, Monroe Harper, however, who then resold the land to Mr. Fall.*[87]

Perhaps the pinnacle of Mrs. Barber's career at Three Rivers occurred in 1902, when she drove seven to eight hundred head of cattle west over the

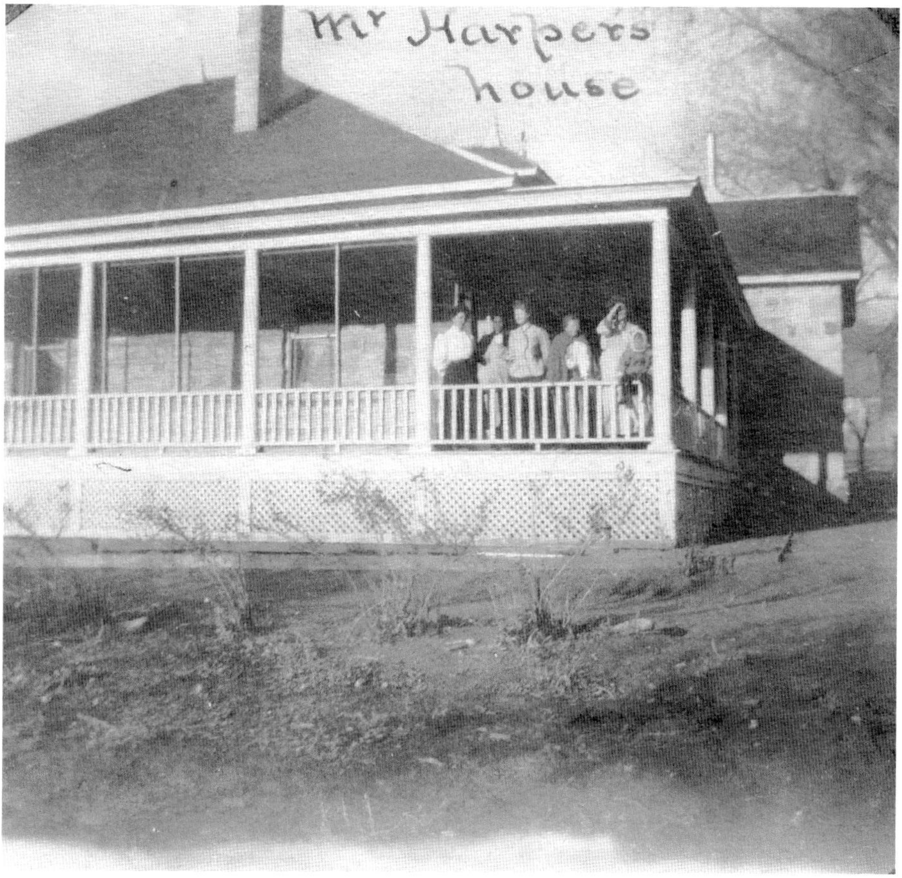

Photo of (Monroe?) Harper home, circa 1940. *Photo courtesy of Tularosa Basin Historical Society, Image P370.*

San Andres Mountains to Engle, where they were put on a train and shipped to Kansas City.

But Susan McSween Barber was slowing down and could not maintain ranching operations. William Keleher surmised that at one time Charles Eddy and his associates held the rights to Barber's Three Rivers ranch, with the intention to continue the El Paso and White Oaks Railroad.[88] She bought out her partners and then sold the rights to SLS to Monroe Harper on July 3, 1902, for $32,000.[89]

Albert B. Fall had moved into the area and was buying all the land and ranches that he could, but Susan refused to sell to him. Unfortunately for her, as soon as she sold to Harper, Harper almost immediately resold it to Fall in two notes of $3,250 each—the first due in June 1918 and the second in 1919.[90]

Previously, as Susan's fortune prospered, she bought mining properties and built a house in White Oaks, which in many ways mirrored her final days. In the twilight of her years, she slowly lost the money from the sale of the Three Rivers ranch. She suffered another setback when, in 1923, for the second time in her life, her home burned and she was forced to jump from the burning building. Again, due to a fire, she was left with just the clothes on her back. On January 3, 1931, after a bad bout of influenza, eighty-six-year-old Susan Hummer McSween Barber died in a friend's house. She is buried in the Cedarvale Cemetery in White Oaks.

J. Denton Simms

In 1905, J. Denton Simms bought a ranch fourteen miles up the valley from the railroad:

> *The house was made partly of logs, partly adobe. It had a sod roof on which weeds and flowers were growing. A large stone chimney at one end marked the location of the fireplace that warmed our living-dining room.*
>
> *A row of cottonwoods which framed the west and north sides of the yard were watered from an ever-flowing ditch. The small stream came from a diversion dam some distance above the house and brought water to irrigate about five acres of alfalfa and a small orchard already in production. The same ditch would be used later to water a garden, a watermelon patch, and other crops as we cleared and brought more land into production…*
>
> *Except for the well-vegetated stream bottom, with its cottonwood trees and willows, our ranch land was mostly hilly and rocky with a sparse cover of arid-land vegetation—live oak and juniper trees, mesquite brush and cactus, and various dry-land native grasses.*
>
> *Our ranch, by the way, lay just across the Otero County line inside Lincoln County. Besides the Coghlan Ranch, a few miles west downstream, there were perhaps six smaller ranches scattered along the forks called Indian Creek, Golondrina Creek, and the main stream called Three Rivers.*
>
> *Other neighbors, the Wingfields, the Crosbys, the Goodins, the Nabors, and the Ellises, to name a few came to be good and thankful neighbors. Many of*

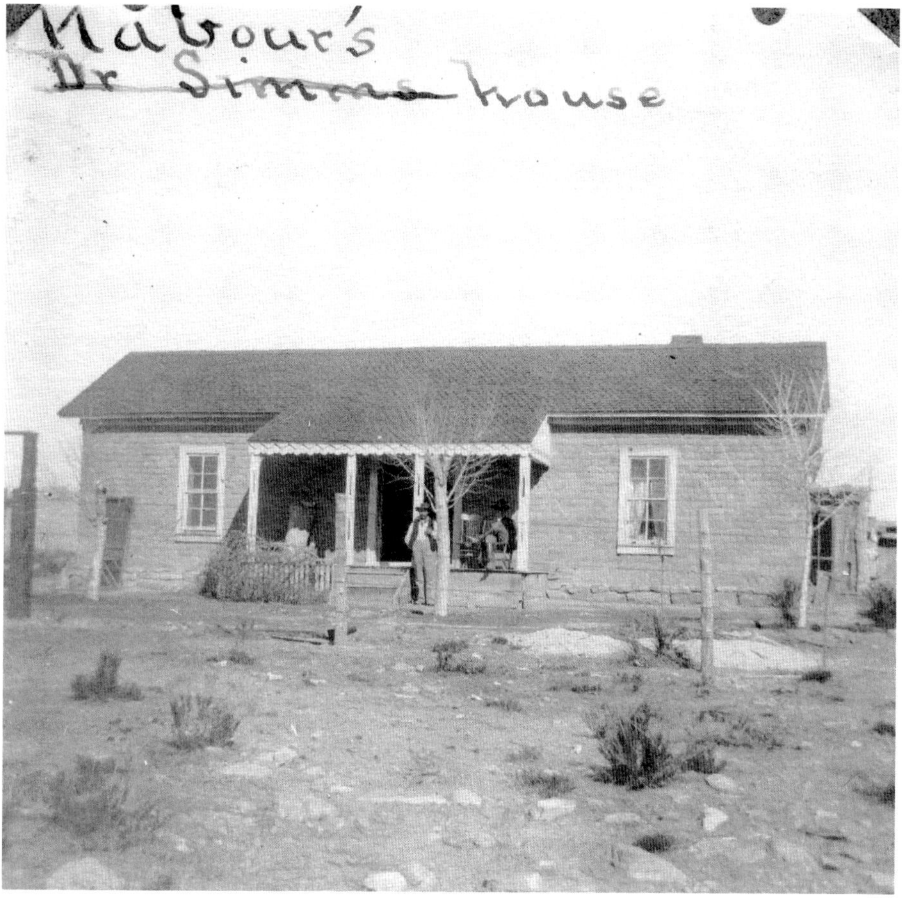

Nabour's, later Simms's, house. *Photo courtesy of Tularosa Basin Historical Society, Image P362.*

> *them were pioneers in this area, and regaled us as newcomers with stories of Indian raids, rustlers and gun battles in earlier, more violent days.*[91]

Life on the ranch was tough for a family moving to an unknown, desolate area. Upon arrival, Mr. Simms had set up a cookstove in their house, and a neighbor had donated a lamb for the family to eat. Their first meal at Three Rivers consisted of lamb, biscuits and milk from their cow. Simms says:

> *This was a beautiful country, and potentially productive, but lonely for a family accustomed to living in a more populous area. There was no church and no permanent school any nearer than Tularosa, 30 miles away.*[92]

The Simms family had bought land in hopes of raising crops and livestock. When purchased, the land had fifteen acres producing alfalfa and a small orchard. A garden was soon planted, supplemented by chickens, hogs and the milk cow. The orchard also produced many apples, peaches and berries and was virtually insect free.

The family quickly expanded their farming to provide crops to other ranches in the area. There were some hard lessons learned, such as the time Denton tried to sell alfalfa that was not cured and had become moldy. Another time he took a large load of watermelons to Carrizozo but could find no buyers.

The family next filed on their 160-acre homestead and, in the process, also filed to use some of the abundant water in Three Rivers Creek to irrigate their orchard and other crops.

To access this water, Simms had to dig an irrigation ditch for over a mile. With no other machinery available than a plow and scraper, Simms finally was able to build the ditch with the help of a pick and shovel. The ditch supplied water to a forty-acre apple orchard that Simms fenced. Once this task was completed, he ordered more apple trees via mail, and knowing it would be several years before the trees would produce fruit, he planted corn in rows between the trees.

The family cleared out the stream bottom near the house, allowing for more hay and garden space, and Mr. Simms filed on a three-hundred-acre "desert claim" north of the property.

In the desert, access to water is always critical. Denton writes:

> *One of the most difficult jobs I faced was the relocating and rebuilding of a diversion dam and ditch to bring water from the stream to a few acres of irrigated land near our home. Floods had cut the streambed so low that it was difficult to get water out into our ditch. To relocate the diversion dam, I had to cut through some twenty to thirty feet of solid rock. I had no experience with rock drilling or blasting, but we couldn't afford to hire an expert. So I bought some drills, a heavy sledge hammer and some dynamite, and learned the hard way. I was making good progress, too, drilling holes for the dynamite sticks which would blast out a new trench. I would hold the drill with my left hand and strike it with the sledge hammer, held in my right hand.*[93]

Soon after the irrigation ditches were in use and a good crop of alfalfa was growing, Simms noticed a herd of hogs belonging to his neighbor rooting up his fields. Simms had been given a dog by his neighbor Joe Wingfield and, with the dog's help, drove the hogs back to their owner, who promised it would not happen again. A short time later, Simms discovered the hogs destroying his garden. He again confronted the hogs' owner, who said he was sorry. On the third occurrence, Simms began shooting the hogs and dragging their carcasses into an arroyo. After the fourth time and more hogs lost, the owner finally fenced his property to contain the hogs.

Simms says Wingfield was a good neighbor on many counts. Knowing that the family was short of food due to the hogs destroying the family garden, Simms said that Wingfield just showed up one day with a quarter of beef, saying that his family couldn't eat it all and it would just go to waste. This act was repeated several times while the Simms family lived at Three Rivers.[94]

As part of the homestead requirements, the claimant had to build a home and spend a certain portion of time living in it, all the while making improvements to the land and structure. Simms was no exception, staying not only as a requirement of the law but also because the new orchard required work.

During the time of "proving up" the homestead, Simms dealt with many wild creatures, including skunks, pack rats that continually took his small possessions and rattlesnakes.

During this time, Simms developed a great respect for the cowboys of the Bar W Ranch, one of the larger ones in the area. It was from the Bar W cowboys that Simms learned how to be a real cowboy and learned how to break a horse, rope a cow and grease a lariat. Simms treasured these associations all of his life.[95]

It was during their third year at Three Rivers that the Simms family met Tom Tucker, a hired hand of Albert Fall whose job was to deal with the small landowners of the valley. A large man weighing well over two hundred pounds, Tucker routinely came to the Simmses' house to warn them against using Fall's water.

Simms kept discovering someone was cutting off the water to his orchard, which he would immediately repair. One day he found Tucker cutting off his water at the turnout gate. Tucker kept calling Simms, who ignored him and continued to restore the water. Tucker admonished Simms:

> *"Young man," he said sternly, "this is your last warning. I'm going to shut that water off and if you know what's good for you, don't turn it back on again. You know Mr. Fall has rights to this water and I have orders to enforce those rights."*

> *"Mr. Tucker," I replied, nervously but as firmly as I knew how, "we've put two years of back-breaking work into this ditch and orchard. All our money is tied up in it, and we have a lawyer's word that we have legal right to the water. I guess I'll just have to go ahead and have you shoot me because, as long as I'm able, I'm going to keep turning it in to keep those trees alive."*[96]

Turner approached the Simms property a couple more times, but he resigned shortly thereafter, saying he no longer wanted that kind of work.

Because of their dire economic situation, Simms went to work for the railroad in August 1907 while his parents stayed on their ranch. Al Bennett, the Three Rivers station agent, wired him, "Trouble. You better come home."

Simms hurried home to learn that Fall's hands had come down the day before with teams and scrapers and had dynamited the diversion dam, filling the irrigation ditch all the way from the river to the orchard. Simms was devastated and went to his dying father for advice. The senior Simms reasoned with his son that no life was worth a few trees. Denton harvested the corn that was growing but watched his apple trees die due to lack of water and the inability to rebuild the irrigation ditch.

The elder Simms died on July 28, 1908, and was buried in the cemetery near Blackwell's store in a service conducted by E.B. Fincher of the Mescalero Reservation. There was no money for a nice grave marker, but a beautiful marble headstone appeared, courtesy of the A.B. Fall family.[97]

Denton Simms moved to Alamogordo to work in the fall of 1909, but his mother stayed at Three Rivers and "proved up" the "desert-entry" just north of the original claim. She hired men to build a small cabin and lived there long enough to qualify for ownership on the property with one spring providing enough water to fill one barrel of water a day.[98]

In 1908, there was an outbreak of typhoid fever at the Shanta community. The Simms children drank water from the creek downstream from the reservation and came down with typhoid fever also. Mrs. Simms nursed her children the best she could but was nearing collapse. Joe Wingfield came over to check on her and told her that a "prominent local lawyer" (Albert Fall) was anxious to get a nurse to stay with her until the children healed.

Mrs. Simms told Wingfield she could manage without the lawyer's help but was relieved when Winfield drove to Tularosa to pick up a nurse. The children recovered, and the "prominent lawyer" even sent up a block of ice to aid in the children's recovery.[99]

About 1910, Denton Simms's sister, Mary, met Fall's chauffer, John Hutchings, and the two married on December 25, 1911. Tragedy struck in 1919 when Hutchings entered the El Paso to Phoenix automobile race with Oliver Lee. Shortly after leaving El Paso, someone fired into the car and killed Hutchings with a bullet probably intended for Lee.

Mrs. Simms proved up the second piece of land and sold both the homestead and desert property to the Gumm brothers, Pete and Roy, and moved into Alamogordo.[100]

Simms concludes by describing the recreational activities in the Three Rivers valley:

> *There was never a day of idleness for any of us at the ranch. Except for Father, who couldn't do much but plan and worry, we all worked very hard, almost all of the time. Now and then, of course, we would have a chance at a little recreation. On neighboring ranches, someone would have a birthday or get married and the family would give a party to which we were invited. Mary and I often rode as much as ten miles on horseback to attend a dance. We would come home quite late, and then be up and back at work early the next day.*[101]

Pedigree of the Three Rivers Ranch

Coghlan's ranch has changed hands many times, but throughout the years, it has been the foundation for other ranches that have also come and gone. A man named Maxwell was one of the first settlers in the area. Though the ranch's pedigree over the years may be questionable, William Keleher has traced it as accurately as anyone. He identifies early ownership from Pat Coghlan, who bought Joe Wingfield's ranch and Bar KL cattle. Wingfield had bought Bud Smith's holdings (the same Smith who later managed the SLS for George and Susan McSween Barber).[102]

When Patrick Coghlan went bankrupt, the ranch was purchased by Numa Raymond of Las Cruces, who obtained it in a mortgage foreclosure and then sold to Albert Fall. In 1912, Fall's son-in-law purchased 900,000 acres of the adjacent Bar W Ranch and merged it with the Hatchet Ranch to form the Hatchet outfit. Shortly thereafter, the Hatchet and Fall Ranches merged into a ranch of over one million acres, or 1,719 sections. In making this new ranch, Fall and his partners controlled not

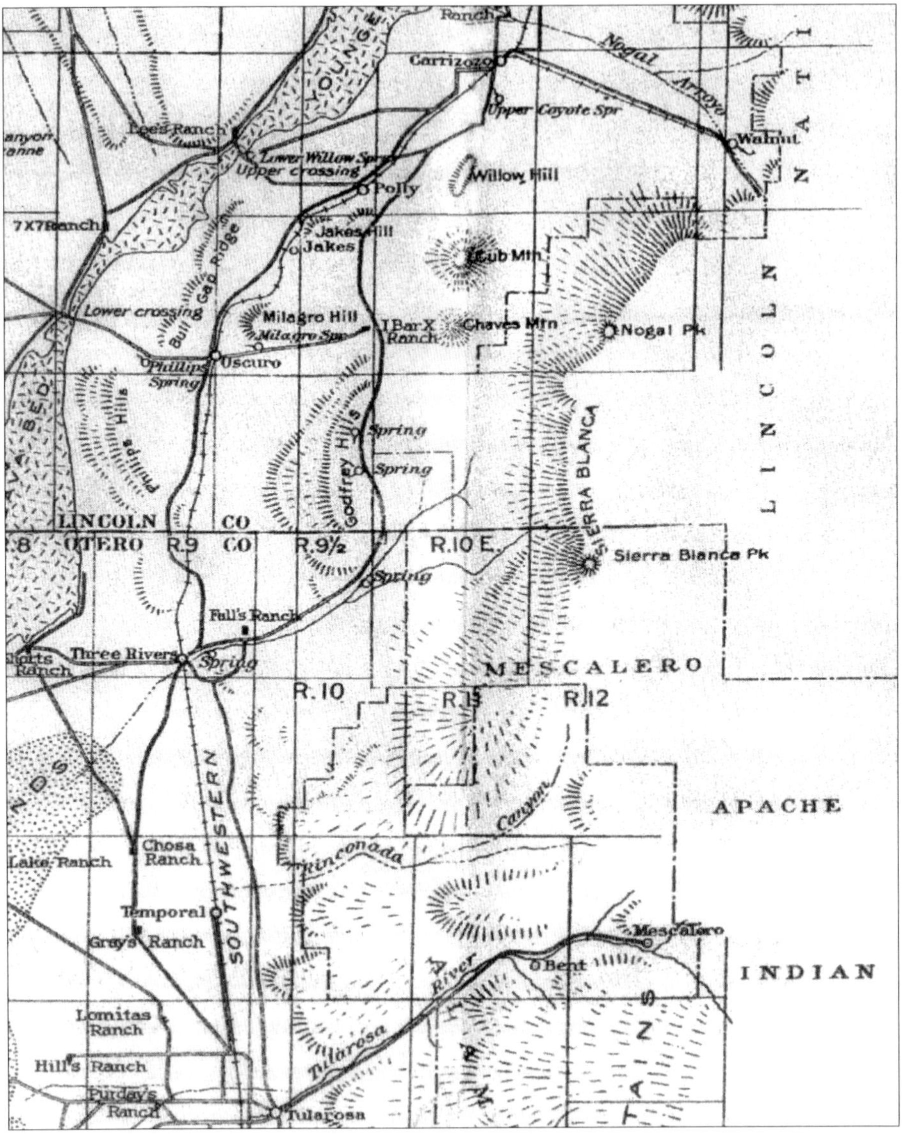

Partial map of Three Rivers Basin, circa 1914, showing the Fall Ranch. *O.E. Meinzer's 1914 "Map of the Tularosa Basin" USGS Water Supply Paper 343 (plate 1).*

only the land from just south of Carrizozo to Tularosa and from the Sacramento Mountains to the White Sands but also all of the springs and watering holes on that range.[103]

4
Albert Bacon Fall

I have known brave men, but of them all, A.B. Fall was the bravest!
—George Curry, territorial governor of New Mexico

In today's world, Albert Bacon Fall remains an enigma. Born on November 26, 1861, in Frankfort, Kentucky, he attended schools in Nashville, Tennessee, and was employed in a cotton factory by age eleven, which probably caused his lifelong respiratory problems.[104]

He met Emma Garland Morgan, a Texas schoolteacher, and became smitten. Engaged to marry another man, Miss Morgan yielded to Fall's pursuit and married him on May 7, 1883, in Woodbury, Tennessee. This union produced four children: John (Jack), Caroline Fall Everhart, Alexina Fall Chase and Jouett Fall Elliott.

The practice of law was Fall's passion, and he studied it as he traveled first to Indian Territory (Oklahoma) and then to Mexico and next to Texas for health reasons before finally settling in the New Mexico Territory at Kingston in 1879. Working as a miner, he continued to study law and taught school until he passed the bar exam in Las Cruces in 1891.[105]

One of the miners Fall befriended at Kingston was Edward L. Doheny, who would later become entangled along with Fall in the Teapot Dome Scandal. Another person Fall would meet was Frank W. Parker, later the trial judge during Oliver Lee's trial for the murder of Albert J. Fountain.

During his long and storied career, Albert Fall was a member of the territorial house of representatives in 1891–92, a member of the territorial council in

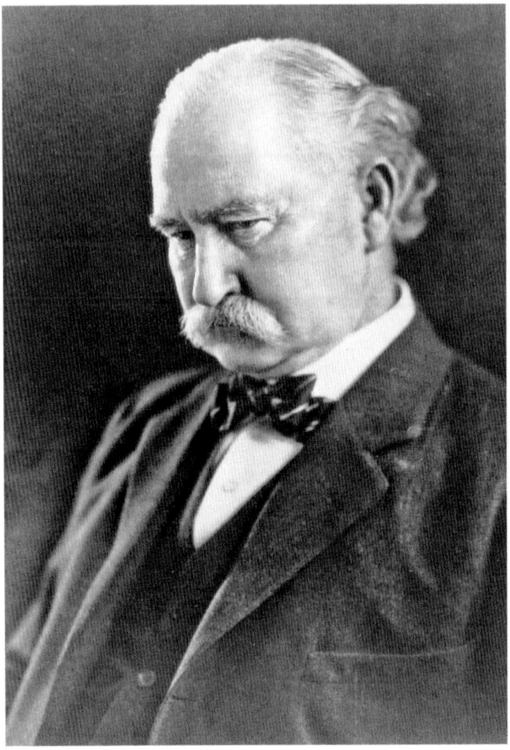

Albert Bacon Fall, circa 1920. *Photo courtesy of New Mexico State University Library, Archives and Special Collections, Image 00080001.*

1892–93, the district attorney in 1893 and an associate justice on the New Mexico Supreme Court that same year. He served on the territorial council again in 1896–97 and as New Mexico attorney general in 1897. As a U.S. senator, he represented New Mexico from 1912 to 1921 and served as the secretary of the interior from 1921 to 1923.

One of the finest legal minds in the territory, Fall defended Oliver Lee, Jim Gililland and Bill McNew in their trial for the murder of Albert J. Fountain and his eight-year-old son, Henry. Evidence at the trial suggested Lee was involved in Fountain's murder and disappearance, but investigators had to deal with a corrupt court system and Fall's legal skill. The bodies of Fountain and his son were never found, which hampered the prosecution. Charges against McNew were dismissed by the court, and he did not stand trial, while Lee and Gililland were acquitted in a matter of minutes.

Fall was a captain in Company H of the First New Mexico Territorial Regiment during the Spanish-American War in 1898 but never left the state.

Originally a Democrat, in a move that became a political bombshell within the state, Fall switched parties and became a Republican in 1902. (Fall said it was because he could not support the free-silver policies of William Jennings Bryan.) Politicians on both sides surmised it was because Fall was not nominated as a congressional delegate in 1900. And Fall was not alone; his friend and neighbor Oliver Lee made the switch with him.

Fall was elected to the New Mexico Territorial House of Representatives in 1912 and then became one of the first two U.S. senators for New Mexico after statehood was obtained in 1912.

In 1889, on a trip from Las Cruces to Roswell, Fall spent the night at Pat Coghlan's Three Rivers Ranch. Telling his wife, "Pat Coghlan's place is the prettiest I ever saw. It's the sort of place I've always wanted to own. Emma, some day I'm going to have that ranch," Fall bided his time for seventeen years until he was able to buy the note on the property from Numa Reymond.[106]

About 1910, Fall purchased half of Pete Crawford's land. The water rights came with it, which he then sold to the railroad for its steam engines. In that year, he bought four thousand sheep, ranging them on U.S. Forest Service land allocated for half that many.[107]

The year 1912 also saw the final expansion of the Three Rivers Ranch while Fall was owner. Mahlon Everhart, Fall's son-in-law, borrowed money from the Thatcher Brothers of Pueblo, Colorado, and purchased the patented land and waterholes on the old Bar W Ranch as well as the 900,000-acre Hatchet Ranch. This enlarged Fall's Tres Ritos ranch to over one million acres.[108]

He did not have good relations with the Mescalero Apaches. In 1912, while a U.S. senator, Fall introduced legislation in the form of Senate Bill 6659, which would have established the Mescalero National Park. The Mescaleros defeated the bill, but two years later, Fall introduced a more devastating bill that would include 160-acre "allotments" for tribal members, with any "excess" lands going to non-Indians. Included in the second bill was legislation that would strip $3 million of timber and allow prospectors to mine reservation land. Finally, land on the west side of Sierra Blanca would be sold for summer cottages. This bill was also defeated. Fall proposed the "Rio Grande National Park" in 1916 and continued to lobby for the park until 1922. Evolving from this idea was the use of high desert land for the treatment of tuberculosis. Fall proposed a twelve-mile radius from the Three Rivers railroad station across Mescalero land to a national sanitarium. Fall was somewhat successful in his idea but at a different location when the White Sands National Monument was established.[109]

Eve Ball, in her groundbreaking history of the Mescalero people, wrote of these times and the actions of the Apache Daklugie:

> *Daklugie was a powerful example of those of whom he spoke. Determined to gain the release of the prisoners of war* [the Apaches being held at Fort Sill, Oklahoma], *he made the trip to Washington at his own expense and was able to win the consent of the Secretary of War, the Commissioner of Indian Affairs and the Senate. The motion before the Senate failed of unanimous passage by one vote—that of A.B. Fall of New Mexico, who*

objected due to his determination to have the Mescalero Reservation made a National Park. In 1912, the year before the Chiricahua release, and again in 1916, Fall introduced bills for that purpose. The year after Fall's 1916 bill followed its predecessor to defeat, Daklugie "met Senator Fall at the [Three Rivers] *Trading Post. When he spoke and offered his hand, I took it. After all, we'd won the Reservation. He said 'I have to hand it to you Daklugie, I didn't think it could be done, but you've won. If his ranch had been at stake the Senator might have understood the reason for our stubbornness and why the Apaches had won.'"*[110]

Fall paid his debt to Coughlan and, by 1912, owned over one million acres from Carrizozo to Tularosa and from the Sacramento Mountains to the San Andres Mountains, where he bought and controlled the watering rights once held by the Bar W to Brazel Spring, the extreme southern springs, Malpais Spring on the west, 7 X Well and Mound Springs on the northwest, Willow Springs between Malpais and the railroad and the lower waters of Three Rivers. Additionally, he added the Upper Willow Spring, Jake's Spring, Chavez Spring, Venau Spring and Vera Cruz Spring, all east of the railroad. More importantly, Fall had extensive plans for a water control system to develop the Three Rivers Ranch, the most important being the irrigation system from Indian Creek.[111]

When Monroe Harper deeded his land to Fall in 1915, it gave Fall holdings of 103,000 acres. The Hatchet Cattle Company bought the Bar W Ranch west of the highway, and it was then purchased by the Three Rivers group. This combined ranch ran over one hundred square miles with over 1 million acres of purchased and leased land.[112]

Undoubtedly, Fall's pride and joy was the ranch house, purchased from Monroe Harper in 1915. The original house used by Pat Coghlan was a traditional Colonial-style adobe but was transformed into the showplace of New Mexico. It was a place for Fall to escape the pressures of Washington and relax.

There was a center hall, and the first floor included a living room, dining room and kitchen. There were five bedrooms on the upper story but only one bathroom. Later on, a bedroom and bathroom were added on the ground floor. A library100 feet wide and 150 feet deep was added on the west side of the ground floor. The room was filled with law books and first editions of other volumes.[113]

In front of the house, a circular drive led from the entrance of the ranch. White columns that reached to the top of the first story lined the front of the

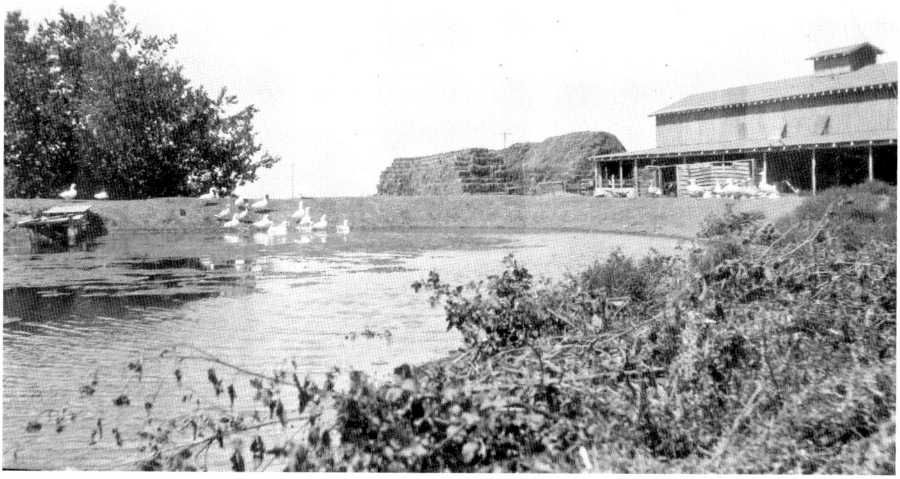

The barn and duck pond on Albert Fall's Three Rivers Ranch, circa 1930. *Photo courtesy of New Mexico State University Library, Archives and Special Collections, Image 00080009.*

house. There was an open porch on the ground floor and a screened-in porch on the upper story, which was reached through the hall. There was a *porte-cochere* on the right side of the building. Surrounding the house were pecan and poplar trees and gardens tended by a Frenchman named Morac.[114]

Mrs. Fall's conservatory, positioned between the library and the added bedroom, held every conceivable blooming plant that would grow in the area, including night-blooming jasmines and even a palm tree, which grew through the ceiling. There were orchards of lime, lemon and orange trees. Catalpa, poplar and pecan trees were added to the native cottonwoods at the nearby stream. A massive barn was constructed near the duck pond.

There was a large bunkhouse for the ranch hands who worked on the ranch and small homes for the Mexicans who also worked the property. During the 1920s and 1930s, it was discovered that about thirty homes on the ranch were causing a large tax burden. Those old adobe homes were razed to reduce the property taxes.[115]

In 1880, the Santo Nino de Atocha Chapel was built by Franciscans to minister to the needs of the inhabitants of the valley. Services are still held at the chapel today on an irregular basis.

Daughter Caroline married Mahlon Everhart in 1909. At the time of the wedding, Everhart was an experienced ranchman and soon joined his

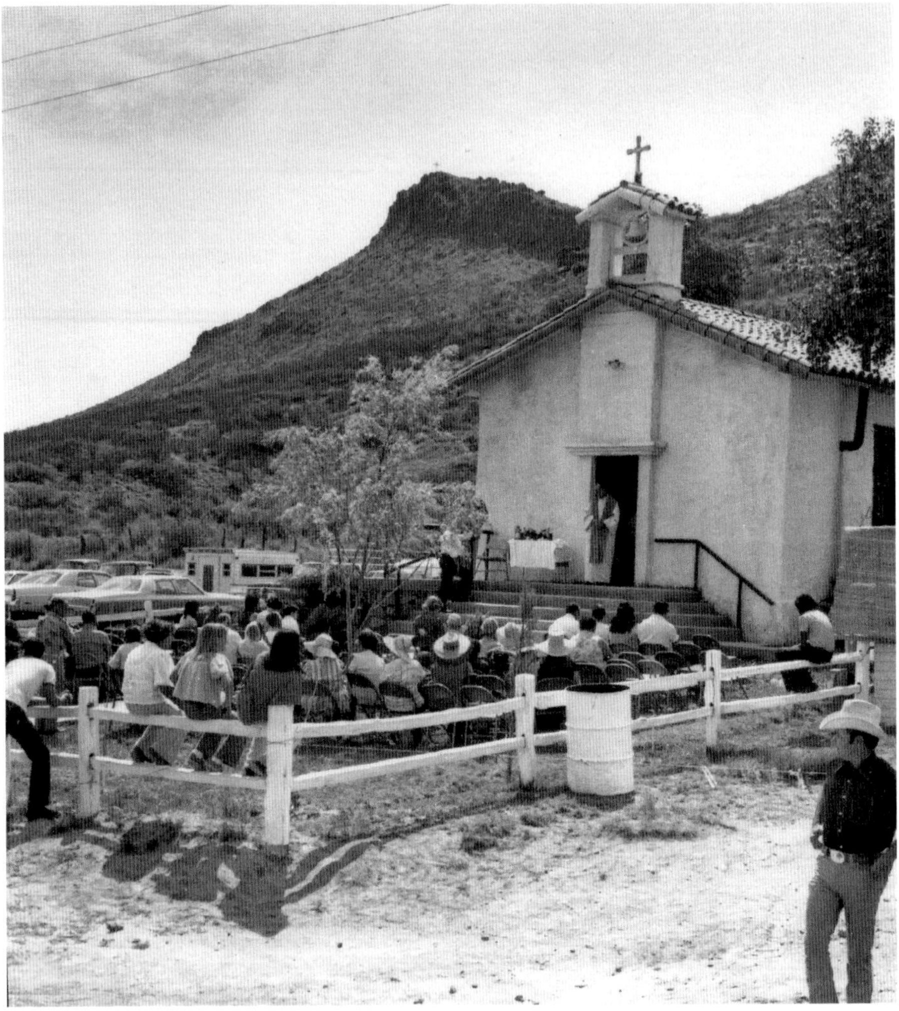

Santo Nino de Atocha Chapel, circa 1960s. *Photo courtesy of Lincoln County Historical Society, Image jst374.*

father-in-law and brother-in-law, Jack Fall, in running the Three Rivers Ranch, sometimes called the Three Rivers Cattle and Land Company.

In 1918–19, the Spanish flu killed 550,000 people in the United States. Fall's son, Jack, and daughter Caroline were among those victims. Jack attended the Republican Convention in Santa Fe in October 1918. On the return trip, he became ill and died in Carrizozo with his father at his bedside. A week later, Caroline became sick with the same illness, which was contracted while tending to her ill brother, and she died in Alamogordo.

Jack's wife was six months pregnant at the time. Mrs. Fall, another daughter and four grandchildren were also felled by the flu but survived. Senator Fall spent his time taking care of his family and those workers living on his ranch who had the flu.[116]

Jack was his father's pride and joy, and Fall had bought the ranch with the intention of making it Jack's. Fall was quoted as saying, "I built Three Rivers for my son. I molded my son for Three Rivers. This vast, earthly heaven—it would have been given him solid achievement all his life— dignity—love."[117]

In 2006, Janie Bell Furman interviewed Fall's granddaughter Mary Chase Roberts, who described Albert Bacon Fall and life at Three Rivers. Furman recorded:

> *Mary Roberts was born in 1922 to Clarence C. Roberts and his wife, Alexina Fall Chase. She is one of those rare treasures of the Tularosa Basin. She spent her formative years on her grandparent's ranch at Three Rivers. Mary fondly remembered Emma had a little service station/grocery store near the railroad tracks. A shelf near the ceiling was lined with copies of the Congressional records; Mary had no idea what happened to them. Emma was also the postmaster of Three Rivers. Emma did not travel with Albert as much as Mary's mother, who often acted as Fall's Washington hostess and was the first New Mexican woman to attend a national Republican Convention.*
>
> *Mrs. Robert's three brothers—Albert, William Green, C.C. (called Junior) and a sister, Emadair—and their cousins, spent many happy hours on the ranch. However, Emadair and her mother spent much time at Fall's El Paso home. Emadair was six and a half years older than Mary and was educated in El Paso while Mary attended the little school at Three Rivers. The one-room school still stands near the railroad, and, today, has cottonwoods growing inside. Mary thought she got the short end of the education but probably had the most fun. The teacher had to spend much time teaching English to the other students. Mexican-American and Mescalero Indians, especially the Shantas, were Mary's playmates. She recalled that she and one of her best friends, Virginia Klinecole, from the Shanta family, liked especially to play on the cool dirt floor, in the Indian chapel. Mary called herself Maryina* [but] *her friends still call her Marina…*
>
> *"Grandfather was Commander-in-Chief when he was at the ranch," Mary recalled. The lane led from the main dirt road to form a circle approximately 50' away from the big house which faced a concrete ditch on the south side. Mary and her cousin, Carrie, nine months older, managed*

to climb on a retired racehorse when they were little more than toddlers. The horse walked down the road and stopped in the middle of the front yard with their cargo. The girls dropped the reins, left by the previous rider, and started to bawl at the top of their lungs. The horse was too tall, and they were too short to dismount. Grandfather, called "Dandy" by his grandchildren, came out the front door and lifted them gently to the ground. Horses were everywhere on the ranch and considered a wonderful part of growing up…

On summer nights, the children slept on the screened porch across the front of the house, lulled into dreamland by the croaks of frogs near the ditch and trickle of water. Many evenings Dandy would sit with them and tell ghost stories. The frogs would find an entrance to the porch, searching for a meal of lightning bugs, and the croakers gathered around Grandfather's chair. The Chase children spent the winter months with their parents in what was called "the foreman's house" about a block away. Unlike the Fall home, there was no indoor plumbing.

Emma Fall's vegetable and rose garden, as well as the tall cedars, remain a vivid memory with Mary Roberts. Albert brought Emma a rose cutting from Kentucky; she planted it near the house, and it grew into immense size. There was a pond in the garden. Grandchildren thought water and mud were wonderful distractions on hot summer days. Mary also remembered Emma kept geese so there would always be feathers for pillows and fewer snakes. Grandmother also kept a herd of sheep and had a herder to care for them. Several people on the ranch tried to teach Emma to drive. She always ended up in the ditch and decided to leave driving to others. This stately, sophisticated woman never drove.

Eugene Manlove Rhodes, New Mexico author and rancher, lived in these homes in his later years. One of the author's friends came for a visit and presented Gene with a Quarter horse, but Rhodes was too old to saddle up. The horse went to Albert Chase and Mary got permission to ride the fancy mount as she pleased.

Grandfather Fall hired Ollie Norton to come to the ranch and build a hydroelectric plant for the whole area. Fall built a home for the Norton family near the plant, and Mary remembered Mrs. Norton made wonderful cakes. All doors were opened to the Fall grandchildren. When the ranch sold, Norton went to work for the School for the Blind in Alamogordo.

Mary's oldest brother, Albert, died on a Japanese prison ship sunk by American forces during World War II. As a young man, he enjoyed trapping and selling pelts. There were always visitors coming and going at

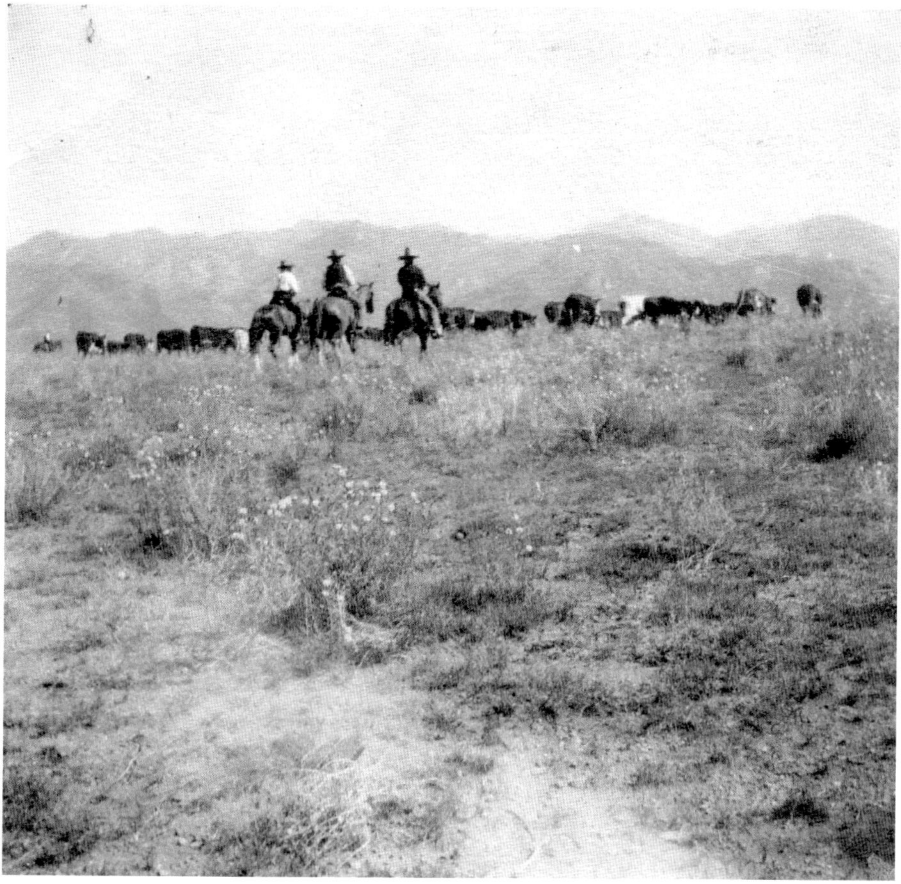

Cattle ranching at Three Rivers, circa 1940. *Photo courtesy of Tularosa Basin Historical Society, Image P331.*

the ranch, but Mary remembered Albert's enthusiasm when a man named Raley, considered New Mexico's best trapper, stayed at Three Rivers. Raley took time to teach trapping skills to the young man.

Another brother, William, was enthralled by magic tricks. He experimented by mixing soda pop and other ingredients, and after burying such a mixture, created an explosion that was the talk of the dinner table for a day or two. William was killed by a faulty bazooka while serving in the army at Fort Sam Houston, Texas. Her other brother, C.C., practiced law in Alamogordo and became the youngest attorney in the Third District to that date in New Mexico.[118]

NATIONAL POLITICS AND THE TEAPOT DOME SCANDAL

In 1912, while a tough, savvy member of the New Mexico legislature, Fall was elected to the U.S. Senate. He became secretary of the interior on March 5, 1921, but resigned two years later on March 4, 1923, due to poor health.

During the early part of the twentieth century, the U.S. Navy converted its ships from coal to oil. To support that transition, strategic fuel reserves were established throughout the United States and designated as naval fuel reserves.

Just ninety days into Fall's tenure as secretary of the interior, Harry Sinclair, owner of Sinclair Oil, and Edward L. Doheny, Fall's friend from early mining days and now millionaire owner of Pan American Petroleum, approached Fall requesting permission to drill Teapot Dome, Wyoming, and Elk Hills, California, which held the navy's oil reserves. Fall approached President Harding, who signed the transfer of authority over the

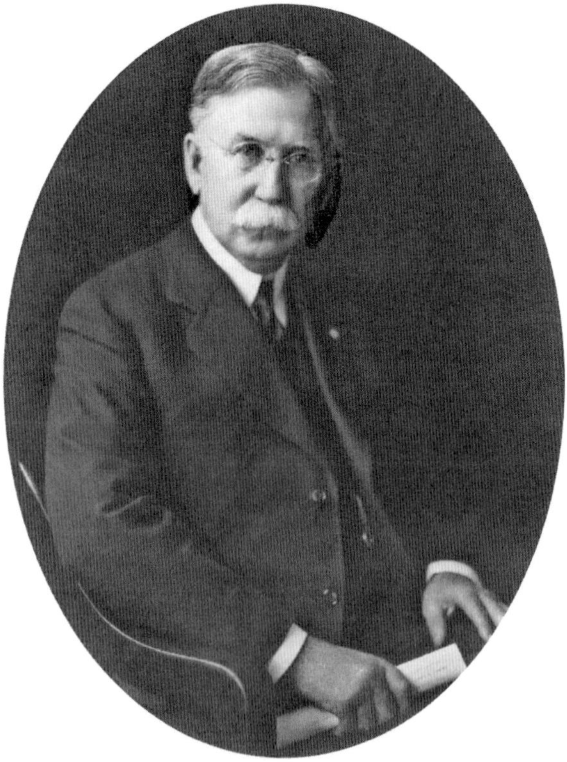

Edward L. Doheny, circa 1930s. *Photo courtesy of New Mexico State University Library, Archives and Special Collections, Image 04640059.*

petroleum reserves from the secretary of the navy to the secretary of the interior. The transfer became controversial when it was discovered the low-rate leases had been awarded without competitive bidding.

Doheny and Sinclair would have gotten the contracts even without the loans because, quite simply, there were no other oil operators qualified to manage a project of that size.

Fall remained in the cabinet for two years before resigning on March 4, 1923, due to poor health and financial difficulty resulting from the ranch. While most people attribute his resignation to the Teapot Dome Scandal, it was actually due first to his history of tuberculosis, chronic bronchitis, pleurisy, arthritis and heart trouble. Second, his finances had been destroyed by the Mexican Revolution, which wiped out his holdings and finances in that country. Back taxes on the Three Rivers Ranch were his third problem.

The Loan

To pay back taxes, Fall borrowed $100,000 from Edward Doheny on November 30, 1921, delivered in a black bag by Doheny's son. Fall signed a note clearly stating that the money was a loan with the Three Rivers Ranch as collateral. Harry Sinclair bought a third interest in the Three Rivers Ranch for $233,000. Fall used all of this money to pay back taxes, repair his roads, plant trees, repair his house and buy and install a new generator. He also purchased the Harris-Brownfield Ranch for $91,500.[119]

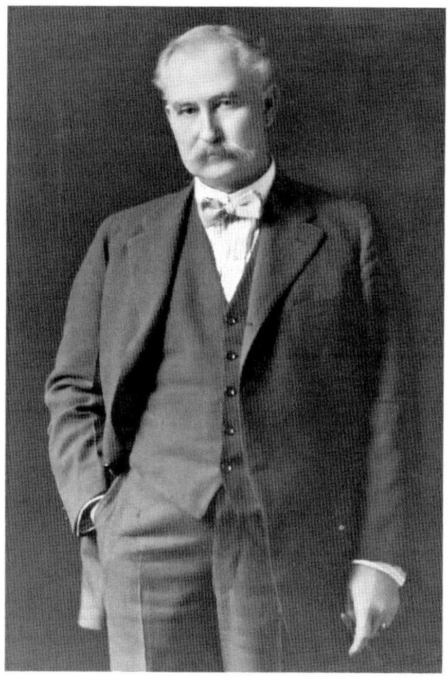

Albert Bacon Fall, circa 1920. *Photo courtesy of New Mexico State University Library, Archives and Special Collections, Image 04640038.*

In April 1922, a small Wyoming oil producer wrote to Senator John B. Kendrick, complaining of the no-interest loan given to Sinclair. These complaints were followed by "leaks" from civil servants within the Department of Interior. Harry Slattery, an Interior Department legal counsel, also blew the whistle. Finally, Carl C. Magee, editor of the *New Mexico Tribune* and political opponent of Fall, began writing of improvements on Fall's Three Rivers Ranch and an infusion of cash in the area. On April 15, Kendrick introduced legislation calling for an investigation of the oil leases.[120]

The Investigation

In perhaps what might have been a case of damage control, Judge Edward Finney of the Department of the Interior announced on April 19, 1922, that not only had the Teapot Dome been leased by Sinclair's Mammoth Oil Company, but also Elk Hills in California had been leased by Edward Doheny's Pan-American Petroleum and Transportation Company because "oil was being drained from these reserves in very large quantities, amounting to millions of dollars of loss up to the present time, by wells on the adjoining lands, and that within a few years the government reserve would be depleted."[121]

On April 21, 1922, Fall responded to charges saying that the leasing had been done without bid by an executive decision because of classified matters dealing with national security. Citing poor health, Fall resigned on March 4, 1923.

On October 25, 1923, Walsh called his first witness in the investigation. On December 3, 1923, Walsh asked both Doheny and Sinclair if they received payment for lease; both said they received nothing, but on December 26, 1923, Fall sent a letter to Walsh saying he borrowed $100,000 from Edward McLean and nothing from Doheny and Sinclair.

Things began to take a downward turn for Fall on January 24, 1924, when Doheny voluntarily sent a statement to the committee confirming he had loaned Fall $100,000; on February 1, 1924, Doheny produced the promissory note for the loan. This was followed by testimony by Fall before the committee on February 2, 1924, when he invoked the Fifth Amendment. As a result, the Senate passed a resolution requesting that President Coolidge appoint a special counsel independent of the Department of Justice to handle the case.[122]

Indictments and Trial

On April 3, 1925, all the original indictments against the defendants were dismissed, but on May 27, 1925, Fall and Doheny were indicted for conspiracy. On November 1, 1927, charges against Fall and Sinclair were thrown out in a mistrial. Then, Fall and Doheny were acquitted on December 16, 1926. A retrial of Fall and Sinclair ended in acquittal on April 21, 1928.[123]

On October 23, 1923, Fall appeared before the Senate Committee on Public Lands and Surveys to explain his handling of the navy oil leases when he was secretary of the interior. At first, Fall tried to conceal his dealings with Sinclair and Doheny and, in fact, perjured himself. When details of the loan became known, Fall claimed the loan from Doheny was personal and not a corporate loan. The situation with the loan was sloppy at best.

Fall testified he had leased the oil reserves with the knowledge of both Secretary of the Navy Edwin Denby and President Harding and that he had done so in the interest of national security. He could not give more specific details because of classified military secrets. Finally, he denied any personal financial gains from the contracts.[124]

Fall's health was already failing:

> *On the day Doheny's testimony* [February 1, 1924] *was made public, Fall arrived in Washington. To the reporters he said only: "I am a very sick man." The next day a subpoena was served him. On February 2, Fall faced the committee. That was one of the most tragic spectacles Washington ever saw: a former Senator appearing before his former associates under what amounted to a charge of crime; a former cabinet officer already plainly guilty of a lie and by all appearances guilty of having accepted a bribe.*
>
> *Fall entered the committee room piloted by Senate attendants who elbowed a path through the dense mass of avid spectators that overflowed the room, crowded the doorway and milled in the corridor. He leaned on a cane. In his best days he had carried one, but then jauntily, as an ornament of his virility; now it was a support of his feebleness. His blue serge suit was creased and baggy, the outer surface of inner demoralization. As he approached the witness chair, he almost tottered; all the lines of his features and figure bent downward, the bars of his gold-framed spectacles made a downward line from his ears to his eyes; the ends of his mouth drooped, his checks hung limp, everything about him sagged.*
>
> *Pulling himself together for a moment, Fall read, in a voice that was clear enough but totally without resonance, a statement his lawyer had prepared.*

> *With the opening words every Senator and lawyer recognized the words of the traditional legal form and knew what it signified: "I decline...to answer any questions, on the grounds that it may tend to incriminate me, and on the further ground..."*
>
> *Concluding, he did not look at his fellow Senators or anyone else. Eyes downward, he turned, took the arm of his lawyer and moved slowly toward the door. The crowd, turning to watch him, was so silent that the tapping of his cane could be heard as, with shuffling feet, he moved slowly down the corridor.*[125]

In his testimony, Fall surmised that the oil either had to be left in the ground or stored aboveground. Even as early as 1919, there was the threat of war with the Japanese, and Fall felt the country would be better served with the oil stored at Pearl Harbor. (A massive earthquake struck Japan on September 2, 1923, that nearly destroyed the Japanese fleet and postponed their plans for nineteen more years.) The turning point came when Fall found that oil companies were depleting the oil reserve at Oak Hills, California, by drilling on the margins of the field.

Bids were invited and three received; none were adequate. (Standard Oil's bid was insignificant since it was already drilling on the edge of the field.) The best bidder, Harry Sinclair's Mammoth Oil Company, was chosen for the lease. None of this was a unilateral action by Fall but included the navy and Interior Departments in the process.[126]

The agreement was far from a sweetheart deal. The government was to receive 12.5 to 50.0 percent royalties depending on the number of wells produced. The company was to build a pipeline from Wyoming to Long Beach Harbor and another to Chicago to connect with a trunk line to the East Coast. As part of the lease, the company would purchase the oil at the highest market price and make available to the navy three million barrels of oil.

Furthermore, the company would maintain 1 million barrels of oil at Long Beach, and a 3-million-barrel storage facility would be constructed at the Panama Canal. Finally, the contract called for tanks holding 2.7 million gallons to be built at Pearl Harbor. These facilities would be constructed and paid for by royalties. For fifteen years, the navy would be able to purchase the oil at market price or 10 percent below market price.

Rear Admiral J.K. Reynolds, chief engineer of the navy, stated that the navy was forced into the drilling program to protect the oil from being stolen. To do so, the oil was put in tanks and stored. When the Japanese missed the fuel tank at Pearl Harbor, it allowed the navy to fight the war from Pearl Harbor instead of San Diego, an act that would have extended the war by several years. For having the vision to make this decision, Albert Bacon Fall was rewarded with a year in prison and the loss of his beloved Three Rivers Ranch.[127]

Doheny's offer was actually the best made, but the way he received the contract was questionable, as it appeared a deal had been struck "under the table." At the same time, Harry Sinclair was given a lease to the Teapot Dome oil supplies in Wyoming. The fact that Doheny made a loan to Fall was confirmed when Doheny foreclosed on the loan.

Congressional Investigations, Grand Jury Indictments, More Trials and Imprisonment

Fall and Doheny were acquitted in separate conspiracy allegations, and further charges against Fall were dropped. However, partisan politics prevailed, and a scapegoat was needed. Fall became that scapegoat when it became public he had obtained a loan from Doheny for $100,000.

Congress appropriated $100,000 for a special counsel, Owen J. Roberts, to investigate the allegations against Fall. Fall was indicted for giving and receiving a bribe and brought to trial in 1926 in the District of Columbia Federal Court. Las Cruces attorney Mark Thompson represented Fall, while Doheny was represented by Frank Hogan, president of the American Bar Association.

Hogan's defense was to frequently object to the prosecution, while Thompson remained virtually silent. During Fall's trial, his son-in-law Mahlon Everhart was forced to testify that Sinclair had given Fall $233,000 in Liberty Bonds and had loaned him $36,000 to pay off ranch debts. Sinclair testified that the $36,000 was loaned for one-third interest in the ranch.

Things got further complicated when it was learned that Sinclair owned cattle, hogs and a Thoroughbred horse at the Three Rivers Ranch and Fall had received over $400,000 from both Sinclair and Doheny. Three Rivers Ranch manager Carroll Johnson was forced to testify at Fall's trial that livestock had been shipped from New Jersey to the Three Rivers Ranch.[128]

FALLOUT

Edward Doheny paid for character witnesses to testify at Fall's trial. They included Felipe Lucero, sheriff of Otero County; Eugene Baird of Tularosa; Robert Geronimo, son of Geronimo; Reverend Hunter Lewis, Episcopalian minister of Mesilla Park; Oliver Lee of Otero County; Mr. and Mrs. Albert Burch; George Curry, former territorial governor of New Mexico; and J. Lee Lawson, an Alamogordo abstractor. Also testifying on Fall's behalf was Father Albert Braun.

The jury was read a letter to the Senate Committee on Public Lands, in which Fall denied receiving any money from E.L. Doheny or H.F. Sinclair:

> *The fact that Mr. H.F. Sinclair came to Three Rivers with his wife and another lady and gentleman on December 1, 1921, or January 1, 1922, just after I had taken possession of the Harris-Brownfield cattle has incited some evil minded persons to the conclusions that I must have obtained money from Mr. Sinclair. It should be needless for me to say that in the purchase of the Harris ranch or in any other purchase or expenditure I have never approached E.L. Doheny or anyone connected with him or any of his corporations or Mr. H.F. Sinclair or anyone connected to him or any of his corporations, nor have I ever received from either of said parties one cent on account of any oil lease or upon any other account whatsoever.*[129]

A doctor and nurse accompanied Fall to court daily. On the second day of the trial, Fall began spitting blood, and the trial was postponed for three days. It was the first instance of the trial's effect on Fall's health, and things would get much worse.

In the end, after what some say were prejudicial instructions from the judge and after twenty-four hours of deliberation by the jury, Fall was convicted on October 25, 1929, under Section 117 of the U.S. Penal Code of accepting a bribe from Doheny. Fall received clemency with a sentence of one year and a day and a fine of $100,000, the first cabinet officer sentenced to prison for accepting a bribe. One person present commented, "This is not the verdict of the jury, but of the court."[130]

The other deciding factor was the public's clamor for a scapegoat for the Harding administration's corruption. Perhaps President Harding summed it up best when he told Fall, "You don't count because you are from a state with no political power."[131]

However, in an ironic twist, in March 1930, Doheny was acquitted of offering a bribe. Sinclair was convicted for contempt and served six months in jail. Also in 1927, the U.S. Supreme Court ruled the leases were invalid and returned the reserves to the navy.

Fall appealed, but two years later, the verdict was upheld. Pleading ill health and a desire to return to New Mexico, he was permitted to serve his prison term in his home state. Albert Fall spent the last few months before imprisonment at his Three Rivers Ranch.

Prison

After eight years of legal proceedings, the key document was short and simple:

> *The President of the United States To the Marshal of the United States for the District of Columbia, and to the Warden of the New Mexico State Penitentiary of Santa Fe, New Mexico, GREETING Whereas, at the July term of said court, 1931, held at Washington, District of Columbia, in said district, to wit, on July 14th, 1931, Albert B. Fall was sentenced by said court upon a verdict by a jury of Guilty to be committed to the custody of the Attorney General of the United States or his authorized representative, for imprisonment in a Penitentiary as designated by the Attorney General of the United States for and during the period and term on One (1) year and one (1) day to take effect from and including the date of arrival of said defendant at said penitentiary, and to pay a fine to the United States in the sum of $100,000 to be taxed, and to stand committed until such fine be paid, or until he should be otherwise discharged by due course of law, for violation of Section 117, U.S. Penal Code.*[132]

Fall's health, always in question, was a concern for incarceration. Four physicians in El Paso certified that he was too ill for prison. Spending a week at the William Beaumont Army Medical Center in El Paso, Fall was found to be suffering from severe hardening of the arteries, chronic heart disease, disabling arthritis, chronic but inactive tuberculosis and pleurisy. Nevertheless, federal prosecutor Atlee Pomerene insisted on Fall's confinement in prison. Fall's attorney Frank Hogan countered that prison in the humid East Coast would endanger his client's life.

The federal prosecutor noted Fall's health had not changed, and he would serve his term but he could serve his sentence "to some more salubrious climate than Washington, D.C." As a result, Fall's imprisonment was changed to the New Mexico State Penitentiary. On July 17, 1931, the United States marshal for New Mexico received orders to take Fall to the state penitentiary.[133]

Ill after the long ordeal, Fall was taken from his home in El Paso to the Three Rivers Ranch on July 20, 1931. The next day, he completed the trip to the state penitentiary wrapped in blankets in an ambulance.[134] He reportedly told friends that while the conveyance he was riding in was called an ambulance, in his case it should have been called a hearse.[135]

Fall was jailed in the New Mexico State Penitentiary on July 21, 1931, at 10:17 p.m. The government was unable to collect the fine, as all of Fall's property had been pledged to the Doheny corporation or had been foreclosed on.

What little documentation of Fall's time in prison can be found deals with his health. He was eligible for parole after four months. In his application for release, Fall said, "My version of the matter is simply that I was not guilty." Favoring Fall's release, the warden of the penitentiary commented, "Confined to the hospital since his admission." The FBI concluded Fall was all but broke, but the federal judge denied the request for an early release.[136]

Senator Bronson Cutting visited his old colleague Fall when he returned to New Mexico. During one visit, he found Fall in a "wretched physical state." Another visitor was Fall's daughter Jouett. In January 1932, a second application for early release was also denied.

Fall's health continued to deteriorate. On April 3, 1932, a telegram was sent to Superintendent of Prisons Sanford Bates informing him of Fall's condition. Bates responded the next day: "If Fall's condition is one of long standing, cost of x-rays should be borne by him. If, in your opinion, he is not financially able and his life would be endangered to wait until his release, you may incur expense and charge in your account to this department."[137]

Governor Seligman received a medical evaluation dated April 15, 1932. It reported:

> *General pallor of skin was poor...Eyes: Pupils contracted and do not react to light...Ears and nose: Poor...Teeth: Gone...Lungs: old, healed, fibrous tuberculosis and Pleurisy remain...Heart: Bad...Blood Pressure: Bad, and pulse varied...Stomach: Bad.*

The report further stated Fall had no control of his bowels and a decrease in his muscles in both arms and legs. He was apathetic, and his memory of recent events was listed as poor, but that of remote events was better. His speech was hesitant, with marked slowness.[138]

William Humphries, a prison guard when Fall was incarcerated, wrote:

> *Mr. Fall was in the prison hospital and was so sick he was confined to his bed. His food was taken to him. There was a male attendant at his side most of the time. To my knowledge Fall had a prison number* [it was 6991], *but I don't remember seeing it on his bedclothes. It was thought by many of the guards, myself included, that Mr. Fall was no criminal and did not belong there.*[139]

Even before he was incarcerated, support for Fall's pardon began. All members of the New Mexico legislature signed a petition requesting pardon and rushed it to the president. The appeal fell on deaf ears. Perhaps the most unusual came from Santa Fe lawyer Francis C. Wilson, not an admirer of Falls. On April 28, 1931, he wrote to President Hoover:

> *I am writing you concerning a pardon for former Secretary of the Interior, A.B. Fall. My action is voluntary and without solicitation.*
>
> *The result of the two trials, one in the case of Mr. Fall and the other in the case of Mr. Doheny, does not satisfy my sense of justice. If Mr. Fall was guilty of receiving a bribe, so was Mr. Doheny guilty of giving it. It may be that the opposite result reached by the juries in the two cases grew out of a feeling that it was more culpable for a public official to accept a bribe than a private official to give one. The law makes no distinction. As I understand it, in order to constitute a crime, there must be a giving as well as a taking of a bribe…*
>
> *Since coming to New Mexico nearly twenty-four years ago, my relations with Mr. Fall have not been friendly. Nevertheless, after mature consideration dating from the day when the verdict and judgment in his case were affirmed, I have had this appeal on my mind…When our judicial system develops a patent defect which casts doubt upon the justice of a conviction, it appears to me that it is the duty of the Bar to endeavor to bring the scales more nearly in balance by an appeal to the Chief Executive for the relief he alone can grant.*[140]

Wilson was not the only one who requested a pardon. Arthur Seligman, governor of the state of New Mexico, weighed in: "I desire most respectfully to request that you take favorable action in the case of

Honorable Albert B. Fall, which I am informed will be brought to your attention in the near future."

A response came from James A. Finch, Department of Justice pardon attorney: "In reply you are advised to date, Mr. Fall has not filed application foe executive clemency. It is understood Mr. Fall has not abandoned his appeal."[141]

Release from Prison

After a year and a day in prison, his health destroyed by tuberculosis and other respiratory ailments, Fall gained his freedom on May 9, 1932, and immediately returned to Three Rivers. The ranch was valued at $750,000, but Fall had no way to pay off the loan to Doheny. Fall was allowed by a previous agreement with Doheny to live at the headquarters surrounded by one hundred acres of land.

Fall lived on the ranch for the next four years before finally moving to his wife's house in El Paso. Doheny managed to hold on to the ranch during this time by lifting mortgages held by other creditors and through a special master's sale, as well as through a second lien by Fall. Doheny next returned a herd of purebred cattle to Fall, which he had obtained in a mortgage sale for $1. Next, he returned to Fall half of the range cattle and then bought 770 head back for $38,500. In effect, Fall had become a tenant, albeit a public one.[142]

After Doheny developed dementia, he withdrew from public deals. His businesses at Three Rivers were operated by Petroleum Securities Company. In August 1935, this company notified Fall that it was selling the ranch property and he had two weeks to vacate. Fall maintained he could live at the headquarters surrounded by one hundred acres of land by a previous agreement: "The order to move came from Mrs. Doheny, who is really running the company. Mr. Doheny has been in ill health and I don't know whether he knew about the letter he sent me [to vacate the ranch]. He and I are still friends."[143]

Petroleum Securities Company vice-president R.M. Sands began action in court by saying, "Mr. Fall had been informed the deal was pending and requested to move. He will now be notified we will take legal action to give the new owners possession."[144]

Fall countered that because of his agreement with Doheny, foreclosure of the ranch did not affect his ability to live there during his lifetime. Fall stubbornly stayed at the ranch. Sands had written to Fall:

My dear Mr. Fall:
We are disposing of the Tres Ritos Ranch at Three Rivers, N.M., and as the purchaser desires immediate possession I am writing to ask you and Mrs. Fall to please arrange to remove your personal belongings from and vacate the premises at your earliest convenience, in any case we wish to have this accomplished by August 15th as the new owner takes possession on that date.

Mr. and Mrs. Doheny join me in kindest regards and best wishes for your speedy and complete recovery.

Sincerely yours,
R.M. Sands

Ever the fighter, Fall responded:

My dear Mr. Sands,
I am replying to your letter of August 2.

We are certainly grateful for the consideration that has been shown us in the occupancy of these premises, but we note in your letter "in any case we wish to have this accomplished by August 15th as the new owners take possession on that date."

In part answer to this communication, [I] *will say before vacating these premises according to your requests prior to the 15th of this month or at any other date, we shall insist that there be some sort of final accounting between Mr. Doheny and myself of all facts and circumstances concerning our occupancy of these premises which you asked us to vacate at our earliest convenience and a final accounting between Mr. Doheny and myself of all matters unadjusted and unsettled between us. Therefore, until such definite and final accounting I must decline very respectfully to surrender possession of these premises to your supposed purchaser or to yourself.*

In conclusion allow me to extend my kindest regards and best wishes for the speedy and complete recovery of Mr. Doheny.

Sincerely yours,
Albert B. Fall

Sands again communicated to Fall on August 12:

We regret exceedingly your present attitude and we reiterate that we do not understand it. In view of your letter, however, nothing is left for this company to do but to enforce its rights to possession of this property by legal

> *process. We are therefore today instructing our attorney to immediately take necessary legal steps to have the property vacated and turned over to the purchaser thereof.*[145]

In the midst of all this, Doheny, reportedly bedridden for three years, died on September 8, 1935. The Las Palomas Land and Cattle Company now owned the ranch. Fall sued to reverse the eviction order. To mediate the situation, the ranch offered Fall the opportunity to live on the ranch for $1 a year if Fall would drop the suit. Ever the fighter, Fall refused and continued his legal recourse, which he lost after a costly legal fight about a year later.

Locals were devastated at the way Fall had been treated. One was quoted as saying, "Nobody around here believes Judge Fall ever did anything wrong. They know him too well…Fall built up this country." And, as late as 1947, Thomas Ryan commented, "You'd better not say anything against Fall around here or you're liable to get shot."[146]

THE FINAL DAYS

Fall and his family went through long legal battles that broke his fortune and his health. In 1935, the Doheny ranch interest was sold to various parties, and the Falls were evicted. The Hatchet Cattle Company to the west was sold to the Los Palomas Cattle Company. Eighteen to twenty sections of the ranch in the southeast corner were sold to Albert Burch of Alamogordo and the rest to the "Quatro Amigos" or "Big Four": Will Ed Harris, A.D. Brownfield, Truman Spencer and Jesse York. The "Big Four" sold the 7 X Well and Willow Spring sections to George McDonald. Al Stover, sheriff of Lincoln County, bought the Old Maxwell Ranch section of Three Rivers. Truman Spencer continued to manage 650 sections.[147]

Albert Bacon Fall and his family moved to El Paso and lived in his wife's house. Shortly after moving, Fall sent his daughter Jouett to the Mescalero Reservation with a request that Father Braun visit him. Fall spoke to Father Braun:

> *"Father," said Fall, "for a long time I've known I should be a Catholic. I was raised a bigot. But because of the lives of wonderful Mexican women who married southerners, I have investigated the Catholic Church. I see the truth of Catholic teaching, and I've prayed for the gift of faith. Will you please baptize me?"*[148]

Because the Fall home was in a parish, Father Dave Kirgan baptized Fall. (Kirgan would later officiate at Fall's funeral.)[149]

Fall received at least some vindication in December 1941, when the Japanese attacked Pearl Harbor. When the smoke of the attack cleared, it appeared that Fall's well-considered plan to store oil there had significant consequences for the United States war effort in the Pacific theater.

After the lawsuit with the railroad was settled, the Falls briefly returned to the big house in 1938, but the ranch was sold to Thomas Fortune Ryan III in 1941. Fall was not told. Emma Fall pursued a pardon for her husband even though he refused to apply for one on the grounds that he had done nothing to require a pardon.

Fall's final years were not pleasant. Fall's grandson Albert F. Chase (son of Alexina Fall Chase) was captured in the Philippine Islands at the start of World War II. Originally a member of the New Mexico National Guard 200th Coast Artillery, he was soon transferred to the Visayan Mindanao Force, where he helped organize the Philippine resistance. Chase surrendered with his unit on May 27, 1942, and was initially held at various camps but finally sent to Camp Number 2—the Davao Penal Colony.

In November 1942, one thousand other prisoners of war arrived, among them Father Albert Braun. Later transferred to Lasang Airfield, Chase boarded the *Shinyo Maru* on the morning of August 20, 1944. The ship's first port of call was at Zamboanga. On September 4, the ship sailed for Japan. Chase died when the *Shinyo Maru* was torpedoed by the American submarine USS *Paddle* on September 7, 1944. Chase was the subject of a remembrance broadcast on KOB radio on March 1, 1945. For his actions while in captivity, Chase was awarded the Bronze Star Medal. The citation read:

> *First Lieutenant Albert F. Chase, on Cebu, Philippine Island, on or about 4 May 1942, when the flank of his battalion was enveloped and its ammunition supply nearly exhausted, succeeded through his cool judgment and determined efforts in rallying a large portion of his forces. Lieutenant Chase's superior leadership served to extricate his men from possible rout and facilitate their withdrawal to a new position.*[150]

From 1935 to 1942, Fall spent most of his time at William Beaumont Hospital at Fort Bliss, the Veteran's Hospital at Albuquerque or at Fort Bayard. When Fall was not hospitalized, he lived in his wife's house in El Paso. In 1942, Fall's friends arranged for both Fall and Emma to live at the Hotel Dieu in El Paso. Emma Fall died on March 25, 1943, at the Hotel Dieu

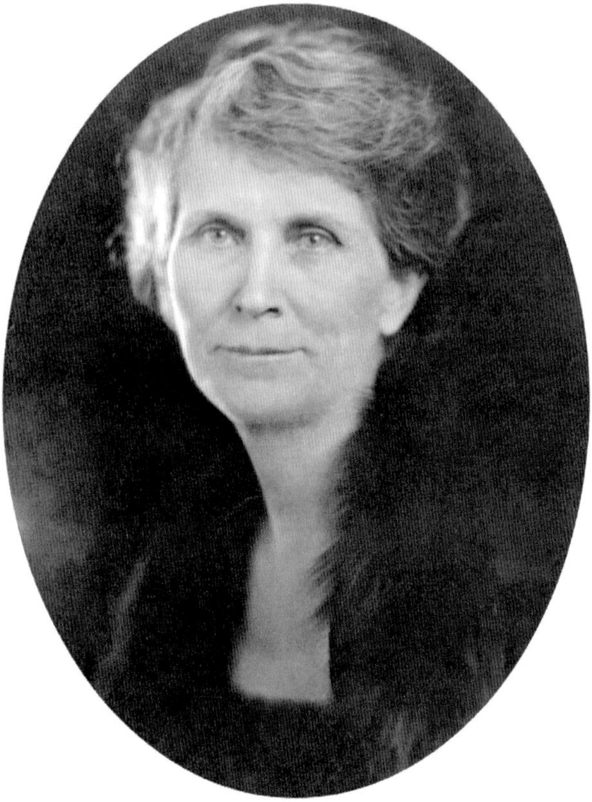

Emma Fall, circa 1940. *Photo courtesy of New Mexico State University Library, Archives and Special Collections, Image 04640024.*

as a result of a stroke she had suffered on March 17. Services were conducted at her home on March 26 by Dr. Reverend Paul N. Poling. Albert Fall was never told of her passing, but everyone thought he knew of her death.[151]

Albert Bacon Fall died peacefully in his sleep at about 4:30 p.m. at the Hotel Dieu on December 1, 1944, just a few days after his eighty-third birthday. He was found by an attendant, propped up in bed, where he had been reading a newspaper that had fallen from his hands. Dr. John E. Morrison stated that Fall's heart "gave out."

Services were conducted in his El Paso home on December 3, and he was buried in the Evergreen Cemetery in El Paso. One wonders if the events of World War II to draw the strategic oil reserve in the United States and ship it to Pearl Harbor made him feel vindicated.[152]

Guilty or Innocent: A Final Accounting of the Teapot Dome Scandal

George Curry, a former territorial governor of New Mexico, stated his opinion on Fall's conviction involving the Teapot Dome Scandal:

> *I found it difficult to believe Fall guilty of accepting a bribe in connection with his official duties. Even now, after the passing of years have permitted cool consideration of all the evidence, facts of which I have gained personal knowledge during the Congressional hearings, the court proceedings, from Fall's friends and enemies and from Fall himself, it remains my belief that Fall was guilty of bad judgment rather than acceptance of a bribe.*
>
> *Fall had reached an age when he saw retirement from public life in his very near future. He had gone as high in public office as he could reasonably be expected to go. His chief ambition was to retire into the life of a wealthy "cattle king" in his home state. He had his heart set on the ownership of the huge ranch he dreamed of in the Three Rivers area. Characteristically impatient of delay, he was eager to complete purchase of adjacent lands and water rights then available at fair prices.*
>
> *It was a terrible error in judgment to accept a $100,000 loan while officially negotiating leases of federal owned oil-bearing lands to Edward L. Doheny's Petroleum Securities Company, and Harry F. Sinclair's oil companies. However, Fall believed sincerely in the wisdom of developing these Naval Oil Reserves by private industry. He felt the oil reserves might be needed urgently at some future, and perhaps an early feature time, and this belief was correct, as later events in our country proved* [World War II].
>
> *While he could of* [sic] *obtained the money for his ranch purchase from several other sources, Fall told me he preferred to accept the loan from Doheny because Doheny was a lifelong friend; that he knew the uncertainties of the livestock industry in semi-arid New Mexico and that he felt sure, if a long term was needed for repayment, Doheny would "carry the loan indefinitely and under most helpful interest terms." This, he said, could not be expected from other available sources.*
>
> *Another grave error was Fall's acceptance of the Doheny loan in cash, lending an air of furtiveness to the transaction. Fall told me he had expected the money to be transferred in the usual course of business by check, but that Doheny's representatives insisted on transferring the money in cash; a fact which should have alerted Fall to the devious*

> *position into which he was being maneuvered. Thus the incident of "the little black bag," in which the cash was carried to New Mexico to close the transaction, with all its damning implications, came into the picture, probably to do more than any other incident in connection with the leases to bring about Fall's conviction.*[153]

The preeminent historian in New Mexico during the middle part of the twentieth century, Albuquerque attorney William A. Keleher, over a period of about thirty years, wrote six major books on the state's history. During this time, he interviewed many of the participants of New Mexico's frontier. In his multiple roles as an author, historian and lawyer, he may have been uniquely positioned to offer an opinion on Fall's guilt or innocence.

> *After having read every available item relating to the Fall case, the writer long since reached the conclusion that the testimony submitted in the various trials had not proven him guilty of wrongdoing "beyond a reasonable doubt" in connection with the Teapot Dome—Elk Hill—Doheny or Sinclair incidents. As indicated by William Allen White in* A Puritan in Babylon, *Fall had probably been induced to cadge funds being used in paying off national Republican committee campaign debts. Fall apparently made the mistake of carrying on at the same time negotiations for a loan from his friend, Edward L. Doheny, something readily understandable by old-timers in New Mexico, and by those who knew Fall intimately. Fall's handling of the business relating to the Doheny loan was careless and inept. The negotiations with Doheny might just as well been carried on and brought to a conclusion in open and above board transactions, without any necessity for a "black satchel." A note and mortgage on the Fall ranch could have been executed and the mortgage recorded immediately in Otero County, New Mexico. The hundred thousand dollar mortgage money might just of well been paid over the counter of the best known bank in America. Fall picked an unfortunate time to negotiate the Doheny loan. Subsequent events in the arena of national politics required a defendant. Circumstances pointed to Fall. He was selected to play the leading role in the tragedy in the trials and tribulations that ensued.*[154]

One last thought: Herman Weisner wrote in his book *The Politics of Justice: A.B. Fall and the Teapot Dome Scandal* of asking Hugh Milton II, a former president of New Mexico State University and under secretary of the army during the Eisenhower administration, to review the draft of his book. Milton commented:

> *You know, Mr. Weisner, I was Under Secretary of the Army in President Eisenhower's Administration. The President, knowing my home was New Mexico, sent a memo concerning a pardon request for Albert Fall. In the memo was a statement by President Franklin D. Roosevelt requesting that Albert Fall not be allowed a pardon for 50 years or more. My answer to President Eisenhower was in the form of a question: How could a man being tried for giving a bribe be found not guilty while the man being tried for receiving the same bribed be found guilty? President Eisenhower deferred to Roosevelt's request, however.*
>
> *You see, Mr. Weisner, I have some knowledge of Albert Fall's case. This manuscript on Albert Fall is one of the most interesting manuscripts I've read, and I've read many of them. I started reading it in the afternoon and did not put it down until I finished it after midnight.*[155]

Guilty or innocent—I leave that for the reader's consideration.

5

The Hatchet Ranch

Located on the west side of Highway 54 is the Hatchet Ranch, which would rival Albert Fall's property across the highway. The Hatchet property was originally the home of a very large Mogollon village occupied from AD 1100 to AD 1400 and is named after that ancient pueblo.

In 1912, M.T. Everhart purchased the 900,000-acre Hatchet Cattle Company and merged with Fall's ranch.

G.L. Tucker grew up on the ranch after his father was hired as ranch foreman in 1948. He states:

> *Fall's daughter Caroline married Mahon Everhart and he gave them land west of the highway. They built headquarters where they could live close to Fall. Quatro Amigos was the Hatchet at one time. Truman Spencer ran the ranch, the other three were just in it for money. I didn't know of the others having any cattle there. All of the owners moved cattle onto the ranch when they needed grazing area.*[156]

On February 4, 1941, the Los Palomas Land and Cattle Company sold its ranch measuring fifty-four by thirty miles to the Quatro Amigos, or Four Friends, all from New Mexico.[157] The Quatro Amigos were Will Ed Harris and Truman Spencer of Carrizozo, A. Dee Brownfield of Deming and Jess York of Albuquerque. Their common link was the New Mexico Cattle Growers Association. The ranch, later called the Hatchet Ranch after the ancient pueblo, was eventually merged with the Fall ranch.

The Quatro Amigos never had its own ranch brand but simply used the brand of its owners' other ranches like the Bar W Cattle that were brought to the Quatro Amigos Ranch during the winter months to graze where the grass and water were better.

Will Ed Harris, son of William R. Harris and Mary Jeffie Saunders Harris, was born in Shreveport, Louisiana, on April 16, 1892. The family moved to the Sweetwater, Texas area when Harris was four years old. He attended school in Durham and Brownfield, Texas.

A pioneer rancher in New Mexico, Harris began ranching in 1913 when he purchased the Susan McSween Barber property, located at the head of Three Rivers, and renamed it the Rock House Ranch. Harris later sold this ranch to Albert Fall. He then purchased a ranch north of Carrizozo but soon partnered with the other Quatro Amigos to purchase the Hatchet Ranch then comprising 650 sections (other sources say 250 sections) and grazing five thousand head of cattle. The ranch ran from Oscura to Tularosa Peak but was lost to the government when the White Sands Missile Range was established.

Harris married "Jack" Reily in December 1925 in Carrizozo. "Jack" was the daughter of W.M. and Nellie Gray Reily, a pioneering Lincoln County family.

Harris was a Mason, a member of the Mounted Patrol of Lincoln County and a member of the New Mexico and American Cattle Growers Associations. He was a cattleman all of his life.

Truman Spencer was a grandson of William McDonald, first governor of New Mexico at statehood. His father, Truman Spencer, married Frances McDonald, the only daughter of Governor McDonald. After Frances's death, Spencer married Kitty Reily, sister of Jackie Reily Harris.

His main ranching interest was the Bar W Ranch just north of Carrizozo. Spencer was sleeping at the ranch on July 16, 1945, when the first atomic bomb was detonated on the other side of the San Andres Mountains. He reportedly said the blast rolled him out of his bed and under the bed.

A.D. (Dee) Brownfield hailed from Deming and operated a different Hatchet Ranch in that area. Jess York of Albuquerque was the "financial brains" of the Quatro Amigos.

In 1948, the Roy Tucker family were caretakers of the ranch and lived near ranch headquarters. They had Brahma cows and many good horses. Much of the water on the west side of the ranch, though alkaline, often had to be hauled to the cattle. Roy Tucker drove an old World War II jeep and would haul a water tank in a horse trailer to the stock. Roy's son G.L. remembered his days on the ranch:

Dad was the foreman and sold his own farm and ran the ranch. We moved to Three Rivers in 1948. We lived in the bunkhouse. Originally it had one bedroom, a kitchen and a front room. There was no bathroom but it had an outhouse. The bunkhouse had a screened in porch. Dad closed one end of porch for the girls' bedroom and made a bathroom at one end of breezeway. The maid had a bed and bath and another room was added for us boys. You had to enter each room from the outside. Extra help stayed in the boys' room during branding, etc. We made an apartment at one end of the building and later on used it for hired help.

There was a yard with grass on the south side of bunkhouse and north of the main house. Cottonwood trees lined the drive in between. It was like an oasis with cottonwood trees, roses, grapevines and asparagus.

The main house had a kitchen, dining room, master bedroom, office, front room, two more bedrooms and a bath.

Dad turned ranching over to my brother in 1963. He leased the ranch for a number of years and finally bought into it. There were so many Quatro Amigos heirs that they all decided to sell it. My brother kept the headquarters and horse pasture. He had six kids and gave each one part of the horse pasture. His three girls lived there for years and finally moved to Alamogordo. It has sold two or three times since then—just the headquarters. My brother finally drilled a well for headquarters.

The Woodside place was on both sides of the road (Highway 54). Rube and Reily McDonald lived there for a while.

There was a long barn with feed rooms, stalls and a light plant that furnished electricity. There was a blacksmith shop with tools.

There was a wagon shed, and two freight wagons were stored there. Mr. Spencer gave them to me, but the store got them and then they went with the store when it sold.

There was also a metal hay barn, which was enclosed all the way around. There were horse corrals between the two barns. South of the hay barn was the milk barn. We always had at least one milk cow. South of there were the chicken pens. West of the hay barn was a big water lock. On the northwest side of the water lock were round working corrals with a chute. South of that was the scale house. West of that was two big water locks and then the horse pasture.

We had a 1946 Dodge for ranch pickup. It had a one-inch pipe cattle rack/side boards. Mr. Spencer promised me the pickup. I never figured the day would come and about a year later he gave me the papers for the pickup. I wasn't even old enough to drive. I drove it throughout high school.

Dad's jeep was like an army jeep. We started out with the pickup, but it didn't have four-wheel drive so Dad went to Carrizozo and got the jeep.

My dad smoked a pipe, and if he lost it everything stopped until the pipe was found. In the 1950s a real bad drought hit and he had bought Herford cattle and then bought roping calves. We kept heifers and took them to ranch. They survived but the Bremmer cattle, and Bremmer cross did better on the ranch than the Herefords. Dad decided to put more weight on the Bremmers and mixed them with Santa Gertrudis cattle. The Bremmer bulls came from south Texas. We ran goats on Santa Andres range until the army took control of the land for the missile range. Dad was one of best goat ropers in the country. When I was in high school he was a county commissioner. I checked things out on the ranch and fixed them and sometimes I missed school fixing things. My senior year in 1959 they fenced the bombing range. We spent three weeks moving cattle to our side of the fence, and I missed three weeks of school.

People would come out of town and their ranches to help out with branding. At times we would have a hired hand.[158]

6

Thomas Fortune Ryan III

Ownership of the former Fall ranch was broken up over the next few years. The Doheny group sold the ranch to the Los Palomas Cattle Company, which sold it a short time later to the Quatro Amigos. Albert Burch bought the twenty sections of the southern portion, and Thomas Fortune Ryan III purchased the main Three Rivers portion. The purchase of $90,000 for sixty thousand acres surprisingly did not include water rights.

Thomas (Tom) Fortune Ryan III was the grandson of Thomas Fortune Ryan, a Wall Street "robber baron" who started out as a tobacco broker and eventually became one of the wealthiest men of his day; he was called "ruthless" in many accounts of his life. Thomas was the son of William K. Ryan, who built the Northwest Railroad from Chihuahua City to Juarez, Mexico. Thomas Ryan was born in 1904 in Chihuahua City, Mexico. Tom's grandfather had mining interests in Chihuahua. Ryan married Alberta Lucille Easton on September 30, 1924, in El Paso, Texas. The couple had one son, Thomas Fortune Ryan III, and two daughters, Mary Jane and Patricia.[159]

Tom Ryan's daughter Victoria remembers her father:

> *I grew up on Three Rivers from 1946 until 1954, after which I only spent holidays or weeks in the summer there. I have some good and some bad memories from those times.*
>
> *After the early death of his father, Ryan was raised in Philadelphia and schooled in Switzerland; he barely finished high school. He was a rebel and*

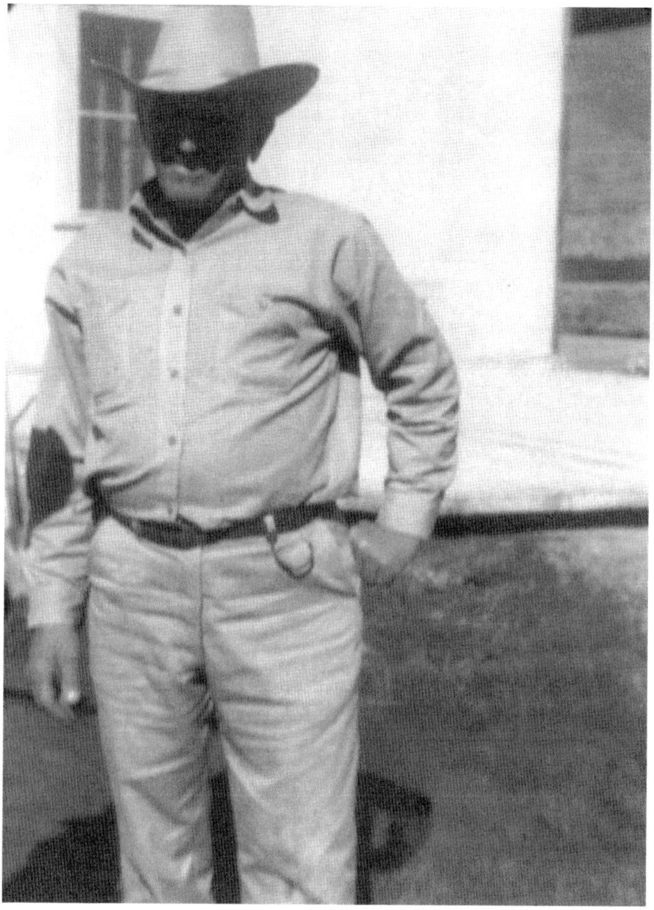

Carol Johnson, circa 1950. *Photo courtesy of Victoria Ryan.*

hated the Eastern society he grew up in. He ran away to Chihuahua at age eighteen or nineteen and thought he was disinherited. He met and married a young girl who was in a Catholic boarding school in Chihuahua whose name was Alberta Eaton. They lived in Silver City and had three kids.

My father did in fact inherit his share of his grandfather's estate, which was around six million. It was a lot of money in that time...this was right after the crash I think. Anyway, they moved to Burlingame south of San Francisco. He lived there until the outbreak of World War II when he went to Manila, married my mom, bought the ranch and changed his life once again. I think these changes in his life were his attempts to get away from his own demon—alcoholism.[160]

After obtaining his private pilot's license in 1930, in 1932, Ryan and five others bought Lockheed Aircraft from Detroit Aircraft Corporation for $40,000. In 1934, Tom Ryan began operating Mid-Continent Airlines with three airplanes. Ryan was chairman of the board of Mid-Continent, and that airline merged with Braniff Airlines in 1955.

Ryan spent World War II as a colonel in the army, flying former prisoners of war out of the Far East. While in the Pacific, he met his future wife, Henrietta Neys, a Dutch woman born and raised in Indonesia and a sergeant in the Dutch army in Australia in 1945. The second of several wives, Henrietta escaped Java at the beginning of World War II and avoided capture and imprisonment. The couple was married in 1947 in Brevard, Florida.

Victoria Ryan continued:

> *He was drafted as a colonel in World War II and did his service in Manila, R&R in Australia, where he met his second wife (my Mom—Henrietta Neys). At that same time he bought Three Rivers and came back from the war to divorce his first wife and marry my mom, had five children (four who lived).*[161]

His third wife (name unknown) was a waitress from a bar in El Paso and was reported to be very talkative and friendly. This might have been "Elery," who had a store at the fishing resort of Guaymas. She lived at the ranch for about eighteen months, and then they separated. Ryan was also reported to have fathered several children out of wedlock with a Mescalero mother.[162]

Tom Ryan III initially made many changes to the ranch, including two landing strips for airplanes. When architects advised him that the old ranch house and associated buildings would be too costly to restore, Ryan tore down all of the Coghlan/Fall home except the library wing and constructed a new six-thousand-square-foot ranch house of Spanish architecture. Also added were a swimming pool, patios, gardens and support buildings.[163]

The new ranch house was built by W.E. "Rusty" Knott and Porter Day (the "official" Three Rivers carpenter) in 1947. Knott's wife, Gretchen, described it:

> *We built another fine house, a rambling adobe that later required a swimming pool, conservatory, tennis courts, a guest house, pool-side bar and dressing rooms. Formal flower gardens were placed everywhere. It was equally as elegant as the Coghlan-Fall adobe, and Mr. Thomas F. Ryan occupied it for the next thirty years.*[164]

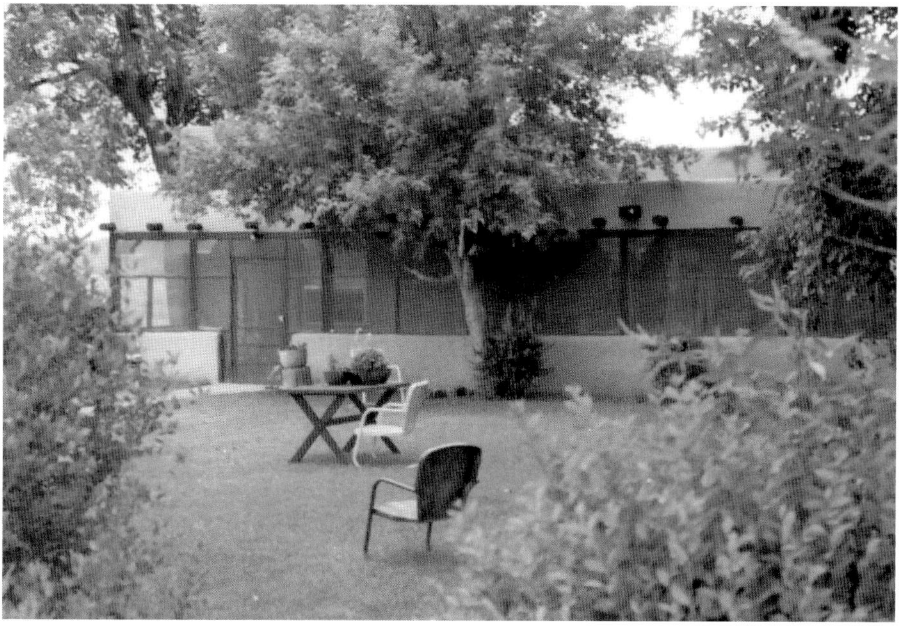

South foreman's quarters of the Ryan ranch, circa 1950. This is the old library wing of the Albert Fall residence. *Photo by author.*

Marilyn Cozzens, who lived on the ranch from 1952 to 1960, remembers:

> *We lived in the old Fall ranch house library. It was made of adobe. There was a smoke house nearby built by Fall and a lot of plants Mrs. Fall put in. Greenhouse—we grew a lot of vegetables in there. There were cottonwood trees, and Ryan put in pecan trees from Stahmann Farms in Las Cruces.*
>
> *Ryan put in both airfields upper* [large planes] *to the left on top. Had to grade it off if Tom was coming in in bigger plane. Lower field was behind his place. Ryan traveled a lot to the east coast and Virginia.*
>
> *There was a skeet range to practice for quail. There were a lot of quail. Ryan built the big house and put in a swimming pool. Tom had orchids in there.*
>
> *Mr. Ryan bought the ranch for fifty cents an acre and put in an orchard. He spent ten years getting water rights—thought of the ranch as a money-making place and his personal escape. He was an alcoholic. When sober he was a kind, generous man, which is how everyone remembers him. He cared a lot about the people who worked for him. Papa* [Seymour Cozzens] *and Carroll Johnson ran the ranch. Mr. Ryan never interfered with them other than he supervised the purchases.*

> *Alison was his favorite horse—a sorrel. Mr. Ryan also bought two palominos when he was drunk. They were a matched pair—Dude and Dutch—and were great riding horses. Someone overrode Dutch and kind of ruined him. He also had a Tennessee walking horse called Bird who was the smoothest-riding horse and a great cow horse.*[165]

An interior designer from New York City, Norma North, furnished the new house with Navajo rugs and Pueblo pottery. While working at the ranch, she brought her two young sons with her who "didn't stop running, screaming, throwing rocks, or devising schemes to drive everybody crazy until they had traumatized every rattlesnake in Lincoln and Otero Counties."[166]

Ryan's house had a swimming pool and two patios in the back, plus a maid's living quarters. A small kitchen opened into long living and dining rooms. There was a breakfast nook off the kitchen and a walk-in freezer. There were two bedrooms plus a master bedroom on the side of the house toward the missile range. There was a long veranda. The house had hand-carved Spanish furniture custom made in Taos, New Mexico, and there was a large fireplace and bookshelf on the south wall.[167]

All but two hundred acres of the one-hundred-section ranch were devoted to ranching. The other two hundred acres supported farming operations. Ryan and his workers installed about 10,000 feet of six-inch pipe to replace Fall's old irrigation system. He also drilled two new wells, and after he hit water at 250 feet, he installed electric pumps. Fifteen windmills and ten surface tanks were also added or reconditioned.[168]

Fall had put in a pear orchard on the south side of the Indian River. Ryan expanded the orchard and put in Alberta peaches. To get to the orchard required crossing the Indian River in a bucket that had been installed by a geological survey group.

While Ryan served in the military overseas during World War II, he hired William "Rusty" Knott and his wife, Gretchen Knott, to manage the ranch. Gretchen (later Heitzler), was a city girl and a new bride. She was not used to outhouses, and the nearest telephone was twenty miles away in Tularosa. Mrs. Knott wrote a very humorous account of life at the ranch during the war years entitled *Meanwhile, Back at the Ranch*.[169]

In 1946, when Ryan returned from World War II, he brought his soon-to-be wife, Henrietta, and their daughter to the ranch. From this union came five children: Irene Ryan, Caroline Ryan, Victoria Ryan, Thomas (Forty) Fortune Ryan IV and a baby who did not live. After the separation of Ryan

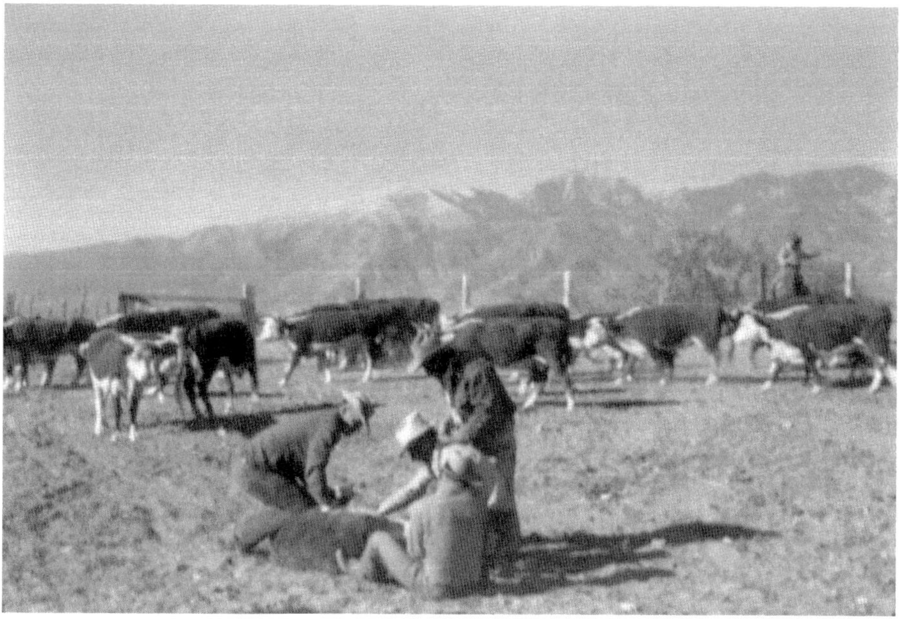

Branding cattle on the Ryan ranch, circa 1945. *Photo courtesy of Victoria Ryan.*

and Henrietta, this family moved to Southern California. Mr. Ryan married twice more, but these marriages, too, ended in divorce.

Ryan built the "Bataan Lodge" on the northern border of the ranch as a hunting lodge for the survivors of the Bataan Death March in the Philippines. The survivors from New Mexico were allowed free use of the lodge and free hunting privileges on the ranch, which held large herds of deer and elk, as well as many bears. Quail were also common.

Among the Bataan survivors who attended the annual activities at Bataan Lodge was Father Albert Braun, priest to the Mescalero Apaches. One year after word spread that Father Braun would be attending, many of the area ranchers also requested to attend, and Ryan approved. One veteran remembered:

> *One group arrived, heard music inside—a Victrola or a piano, I don't remember just what—and a lot of clapping and whistling. A rancher knocked on the door: no one answered—the music continued and he knocked louder, and finally pounded until someone answered the door.*
>
> *There was Father Albert, a derby on his head and a cane in his hand, dancing an Irish jig. Like a true vaudeville trouper, he finished the dance before he came over to greet his old friends with a shout and a healthy* abrazo.[170]

THE BILLY THE KID RODEO

Ryan also built the A.B. Fall Rodeo Arena just west of his ranch house. The arena was home to the popular annual Billy the Kid Rodeo, cosponsored by the Tularosa Lions Club. Rodeo director Carroll Johnson provided a first-class rodeo in which children from Tularosa and within a one-hundred-mile radius participated in the one-day event. The Lions Club hosted a big barbecue at the end of the event with beeves supplied by Ryan. Unfortunately, the rodeo ground is now torn down.[171]

G.L. Tucker was a participant of the rodeo at its inception:

> *The rodeo first started by Tom Ryan and the Tularosa Lions Club was held out at the old schoolhouse by the road fork to the reservation. The rodeo was held there for a couple of years and then Mr. Ryan built the arena above the gatehouse. Carroll Johnson would gather ranch stock. All they had for rodeo stock was calves and yearling. There was no big stock as the rodeo was for ages sixteen and under who lived in Lincoln and Otero Counties. The Lions Club would barbeque beef that Ryan donated. The rodeo started at eight or nine o'clock in the morning and stopped at noon for the meal. Then it started again after the meal. People would park their cars around the arena to watch. Governors Mechem and Simms came to watch. The first rodeo was held about 1948 and ended in the early '60s.*[172]

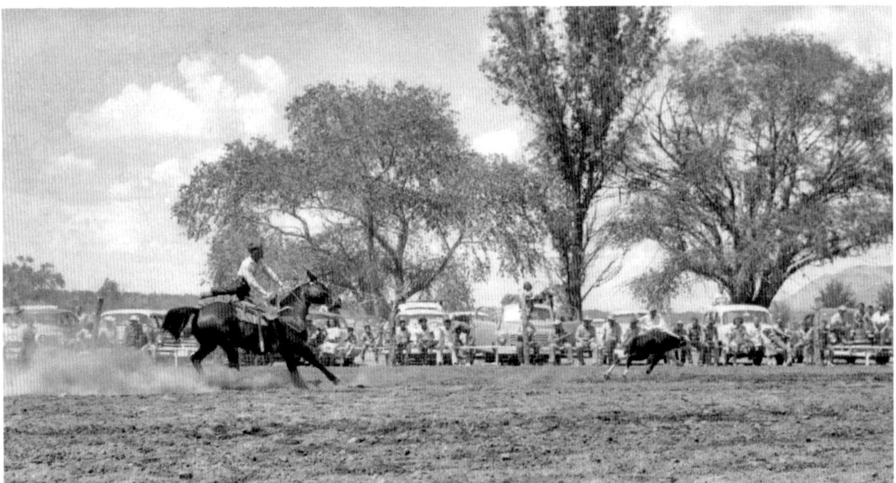

G.L. Tucker on "Old Joe" at the Three Rivers Rodeo in August 1954. *Photo courtesy of G.L. Tucker.*

There were several memorable and comical incidents on the ranch. Marilyn Cozzens remembers one involving burros:

> *One Sunday morning, Papa gets a phone call. I heard him say on the phone "You did what, they're coming when?" It seems Mr. Ryan had purchased three semi-trailer loads of burros in Juarez on Saturday night. The phone call was to let Papa know they were on their way to Three Rivers. Some got loose. Some were sold. Some had distemper. The remainder were sold off. They weren't good for much; we would try to ride them. They were kept in the corrals. We had to feed them.*[173]

The foreman of the ranch for both Albert Fall and Thomas Ryan was Carroll Johnson, who worked for the two men for over forty years, first as a cowboy for thirteen years and then as ranch manager for thirty more. Johnson was born at Nogal after his father, Pete Johnson, came to Carrizozo in a covered wagon in 1887 as boss of the Bar W. Ryan was reported to have said, "Carroll is not only the best stockman in this county but is also my best friend." Johnson died on January 31, 1960. Victoria Ryan said, "I remember he used to take us for rides when we were there visiting in the summers. I remember he smoked like Bull Durham and could ride and roll a cigarette at the same time!"[174]

Gretchen Heitzler spent the Word War II years at the ranch and recalls Johnson:

> *Carroll Johnson, our cattle foreman, was Mr. Three Rivers. He had been born in the area and had lived there all his life. Naturally, he had punched cows for Albert Fall.*
>
> *Carroll looked like a cowboy ought to look, sandy hair, blue eyes, weather-beaten skin; and although he was lame, he moved with the grace and a poise of a person in complete harmony with himself, and so he was. People with this trait tend to attract friendship with others and everyone in Lincoln and Otero Counties loved Carroll.*[175]

Carroll had hurt his hip in a horse accident, and one leg was shorter than the other, causing him to walk with a limp. Even being handicapped, he was a good horseman. He was an old-time rancher, very kind and friendly and outgoing.

Ross McDonald and his wife, Carmen, had their ranch on the missile range confiscated by the government. They came to Three Rivers, and McDonald

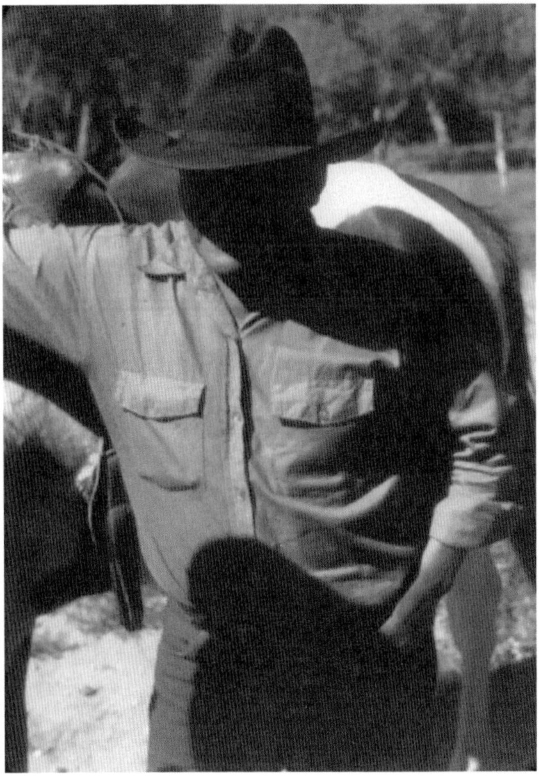

Joe Shanta Jr., circa 1945. *Photo courtesy of Victoria Ryan.*

worked for Carroll; Carmen McDonald also cooked. Their son, Howard, was about ten years old in 1950.

Seymour M. "Primo" Cozzens was the foreman of the lower part of the ranch in charge of farming operations from 1952 to 1962 and responsible for the headquarters and farming operation, the orchards and the alfalfa field. He farmed between the house and the rodeo arena. He was also Ryan's assistant when Ryan was at the ranch. He took care of all of the engines that generated electricity until the electric lines were put in. The Cozzens family lived in the old library of the former Albert Fall house near the new Ryan mansion.

Cozzens and Johnson complemented each other well. On their time off, they even played dominos together.

Marilyn Cozzens continued:

> *Carroll was in charge of the upper ranch/cattle. It seemed like close to one thousand head of cows and twenty bulls. Mr. Ryan owned 110 sections. After he got water rights, there were no problems. Papa got some sheep. Branding was a big operation, and neighbors and extra hired hands helped. It happened in May and June. In fall, they gathered the calves and brought them to headquarters and weighed them. The original corral was rock and built by A.B. Fall. Ryan put in a stallion barn. The bunkhouse behind that was built by A.B. Fall.*[176]

Ryan sold Three Rivers Ranch in 1974 and retired to a five-acre parcel in Mesilla to raise quarter horses. He died at age eighty-nine at Memorial

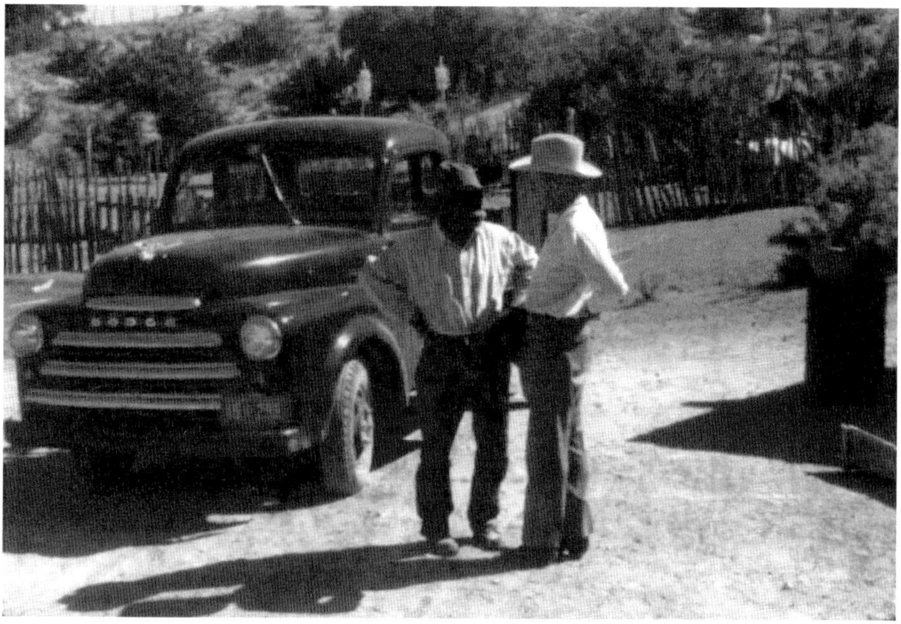

Pete Crawford and Tom Ryan, circa 1945. *Photo courtesy of Victoria Ryan.*

Medical Center in Las Cruces on March 10, 2012, from complications following abdominal surgery.

Few families still resided up and down the little valley that, at one time, was home for seventy-eight families or about three hundred people who had raised cattle on public land fifty years earlier. One of the most popular residents of old Three Rivers was a black cowboy named Pete Crawford. Crawford (1883–1974) owned a home north of the church and is buried in the Three Rivers Cemetery. His father had come to the region as a buffalo soldier during the Lincoln County War and stayed. Another old-timer was Domingo Montoya, born at Three Rivers about 1870.[177]

About 1940, Charlie Trammell and his wife, Threva Mae, moved from their place near Oro Grande to a section of land with a farm, land and a stream at Three Rivers. Acquired from a Mrs. Edwards, the ranch had previously been owned by a Mr. Simms who had drugstores in Alamogordo, Tularosa and Carrizozo.

By this time, the Trammells owned ten to fifteen milk cows and marketed milk and cream from the rail station at Three Rivers to Raton and Trinidad, Colorado, three days a week in refrigerated containers via the railroad.

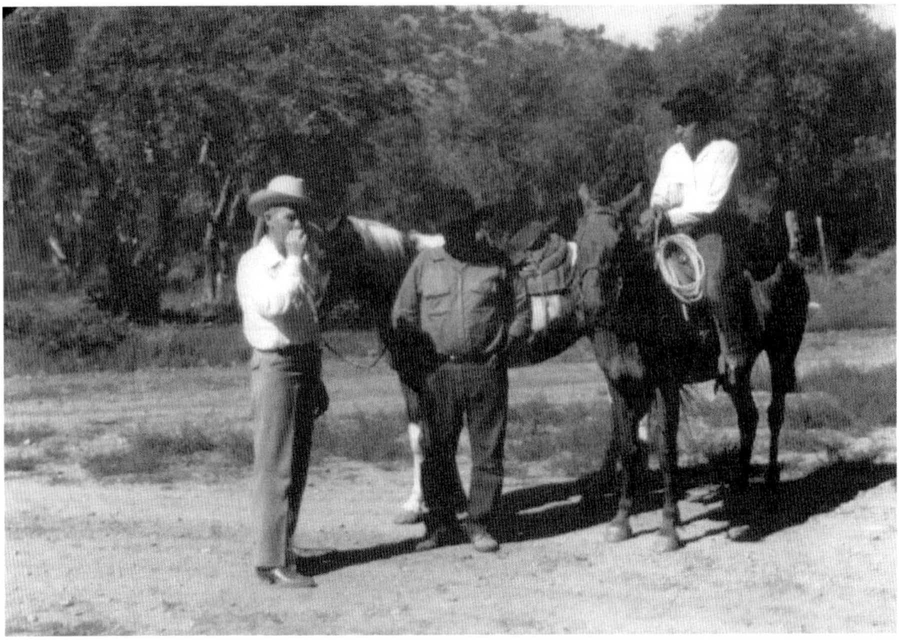

Tom Ryan, Joe Shanta Jr., and unknown, circa 1945. *Photo courtesy of Victoria Ryan.*

During this period, when trains used steam engines, Three Rivers was a stop to take on water. Primarily a depot, the building had rooms for the agent on the top floor. The nearby post office was operated by a man named Woodside. At this time, six or seven families lived here. A water tank and the trading post/gas station completed the little community.

The school, originally built at the turn of the century as a three-room schoolhouse, was located behind the trading post. By the early 1940s, it held first through fifth grades. Older children were bused to Tularosa. A bus ran from near the mountain down to the school and picked up students along the way and made the reverse trip at the end of the school day.[178]

7

The Three Rivers Aqueduct

Fall knew soon after the purchase of the one-million-acre ranch that he needed water to realize his dream. In 1910, an agreement between Fall and James Carroll, BIA (Bureau of Indian Affairs) agent for the Mescalero Apache Reservation, allowed Fall to construct a cement irrigation ditch through the Mescalero Reservation to his ranch.

The ditch would convey water from the mouth of Indian Creek to the canyon to irrigable lands, including those of the Mescaleros. The agreement signed by Fall, binding on him, as well as his heirs, successors and assigns, stipulated: the ditch must be substantially constructed and able to carry five cubic feet of water a second; the head gates were to be placed at the Mescalero superintendent's direction; if fenced, the ditch must be able to water Mescalero stock; the Mescaleros were to have full access to water every other week from 6:00 a.m. on Monday to 6:00 p.m. on Saturday; and work must be started within a year and completed the following year.[179]

Even though Fall had access to the water for eight days straight and every night, the water often froze during winter and dried up during the summer. As a result, he built two reservoirs, the larger holding 500,000 gallons. This allowed him enough water for his own needs and water to the El Paso and Northeastern (EPNE) Railroad.[180] In doing so, he replaced nine miles of open ditch with four-inch steel pipe extending from the Three Rivers station to a reservoir on the edge of the Mescalero Reservation.[181]

On January 20, 1920, the Falls sold their water rights to the EPNE Railroad for $45,000. The railroad was guaranteed seventy-five thousand

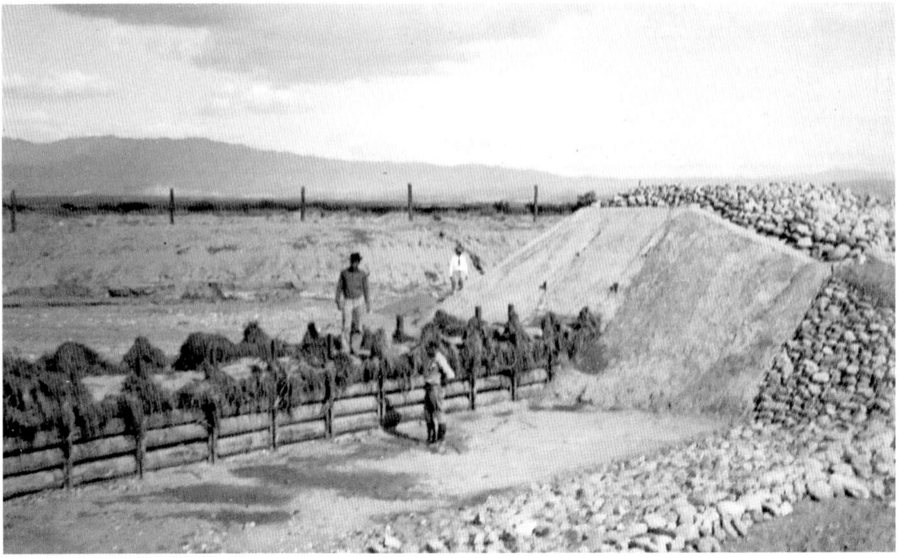

Messrs. Casey and Angle at Three Rivers Arroyo Diversion, August 1936. *Photo courtesy of New Mexico State University Library, Archives and Special Collections, Image 00941536.*

gallons a day, while the Falls retained five thousand gallons a day for ranch use to be accessed at two points along the pipeline.[182]

The railroad soon found out the makeup of Albert Fall after superintendent of water and fuel C.M. Cluff and Floy Skinner took a shovel up to Indian Creek to change the channel. They were met by Fall and his daughter Alexina Chase. When Fall asked the railroad men what they were doing, they responded that they were trying to change the channel. Fall responded, "When you spend as much money as I have trying to change this channel you will find you don't know a damn thing about it. Now I suggest you get that damn shovel off my property."[183]

Fall next installed a diesel power plant about five miles upriver from his ranch house. He also built a fishing hut over Indian Creek, complete with a balcony between the power plant and big house. Fingerlings were stocked in the creek and grew so quickly that the spot was thought to be radioactive.[184]

In 1927, Mrs. Fall requested water be connected to their store. The request was denied because of fear that if this request was granted, many other ranchers in the valley would also want to make connection to the water line. It required three years to resolve this request, and during this time, the Falls carried water from their residence to the store.

Water for the swimming pool at the residence (in reality, an earthen stock tank) was even more contentious. Fall had made an unauthorized cut in the line to fill the pool. A.B. Zumwalt and Floy Skinner were contemplating installing a meter on the line to the swimming pool but reconsidered when they realized that if they did so, they would have to put meters on the whole of the Three Rivers pipeline. In the end, the cut was removed and the pipeline put back in its original condition.[185]

In 1930, Edward Doheny transferred Fall's $100,000 to the Petroleum Securities Company. The company took control of the ranch and hired its own person to manage the ranch. Mrs. Fall was allowed to live in the ranch house.[186]

By this time, the mechanics of the pipeline built in 1916 had become complex. One of the 500,000-gallon tanks started leaking up to 90,000 gallons a day. A question on ownership of the tank ensued between the Southern Pacific Railroad and the Petroleum Securities Company. Railroad attorney W.A. Hawkins wrote on February 13, 1932, that the reservoir belonged to Fall and his family. However, another letter written by Fall in 1927 stated the reservoir had been turned over to the railroad.

The railroad offered Petroleum Securities the opportunity to repair the water line on the condition that, if it did so, the railroad would take over the line based on agreements with Fall in the 1920s.

In December 1932, the railroad repaired the line but did not press the ownership issue. The railroad and Petroleum Securities came to agreement with every party and signed, with the exception of Mrs. Fall. She finally signed on April 10, 1933. As a result, the railroad finally became recognized as owner of the line and completed repairs to the line on March 9, 1934.[187]

By 1936, the Los Palomas Land and Cattle Company and Petroleum Securities both wanted ownership of ranch house, and both entities tried to buy it. When the Falls wouldn't sell, the securities company tried to sue and evict the Falls, but the cattle company would not join the litigation. When the Los Palomas Land and Cattle Company offered to lease the house to the Fall family for one dollar a year, Mrs. Fall refused the offer and moved in with daughter Mrs. Alec Chase next door to her at Three Rivers.

Next, Mrs. Fall tried to change the connection from her house to her daughter's house. Under the original agreement, the Falls were entitled to two connections to the irrigation line. By moving the main house from a connection to a well, the change seemed reasonable. The railroad did not want to get involved in local problems and declined to make the change. Since Mrs. Chase was unable to get water to her house, she moved her family to a building near the trading post.[188]

The lawsuit was settled on December 3, 1936, and the Falls retained possession of the house. At that time, Mrs. Fall was a patient in the William Beaumont Hospital in El Paso. Terms of the settlement were not announced, but it was rumored the railroad settled due to Mrs. Fall's bad health.[189]

Since the Mescaleros had first right to the water, problems eventually developed with the railroads, and a lack of trust evolved. On May 23, 1936, the Southern Pacific Railroad made an agreement with Joe Shanta to patrol the ditch and monitor the flow of water for twenty dollars a month. This agreement ended problems with the Mescaleros.[190]

In 1938, Mrs. Fall moved back into the ranch house and rented her daughter's house to Lester Greer. She again had two connections to the water line. At the end of 1938, the Los Palomas Land and Cattle Company laid a new pipeline and cut the old railroad's line. The next week, the Hueco Cattle Company (owned by Petroleum Securities) wanted a tap. The Falls were entitled to two taps, so the situation reverted back to the old Doheny foreclosure. A month later, the railroad told the Falls that the Hueco Company was entitled to the water.[191]

Note: In preparation for this book, the author visited the site with G.L. Tucker, who related:

> *The irrigation system pipeline went from Ryan's gatehouse to the ranch headquarters. When the Bonito pipeline came through, we got water off that. The railroad and Mr. Fall had built a cement ditch from the Shanta community to Three Rivers to furnish water for the train.*[192]

8

Recent History

In the early part of the twentieth century, about 300 people at Three Rivers lived in the live oaks east of the Santo Nino de Atocha Catholic Chapel three miles from the present site. A post office was established, and a school was built about 1883. By 1890, there was a population of 163, most of whom worked for the El Paso and Northeastern Railroad.

With the arrival of the El Paso and Northeastern Railroad, the town moved to its current location by the railroad. At one time, it boasted a train depot, hotel, saloon, school and houses for the railroad workers. All the while, there were hundreds of houses in the Three Rivers valley in addition to the big ranch operated by Thomas Ryan III. The village reached its peak population in the 1920s. G.L. Tucker remembers:

> *There used to be several houses all up and down the railroad at the new Three Rivers settlement. Family houses were on east side of railroad, and the highway came up the west side. Fall had them take the houses down to avoid taxes. At one time, there was a fifty-five-passenger bus that came from Three Rivers to Tularosa. There was a railroad section house. Cattle were shipped out of stock pens there. There was the C.C. Chase house, the "Hop" Hopkins house,* [an] *old store. In 1948, they changed the highway to the present location, and Hopkins built the current store.*[193]

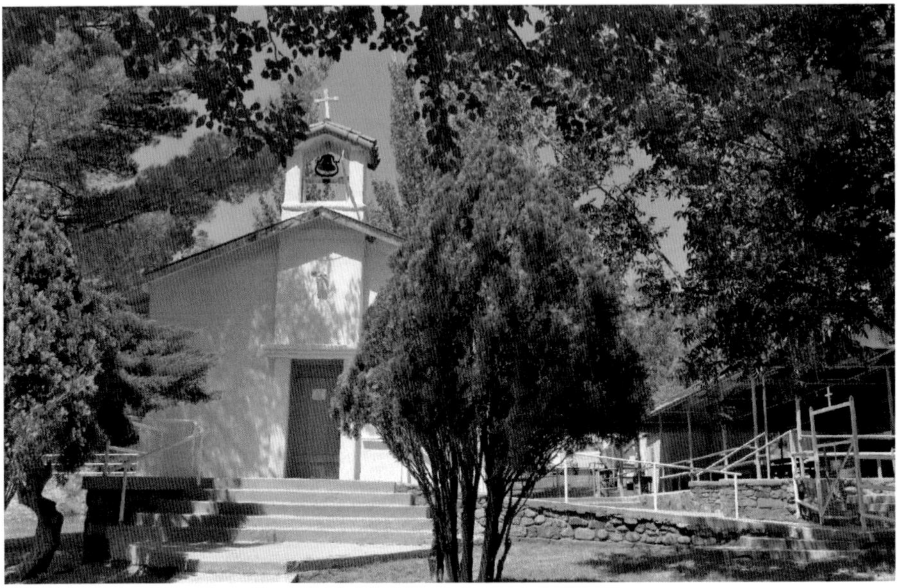

Santo Nino de Atocha Catholic Chapel, 2012. *Photo courtesy of Doyle Cozzens.*

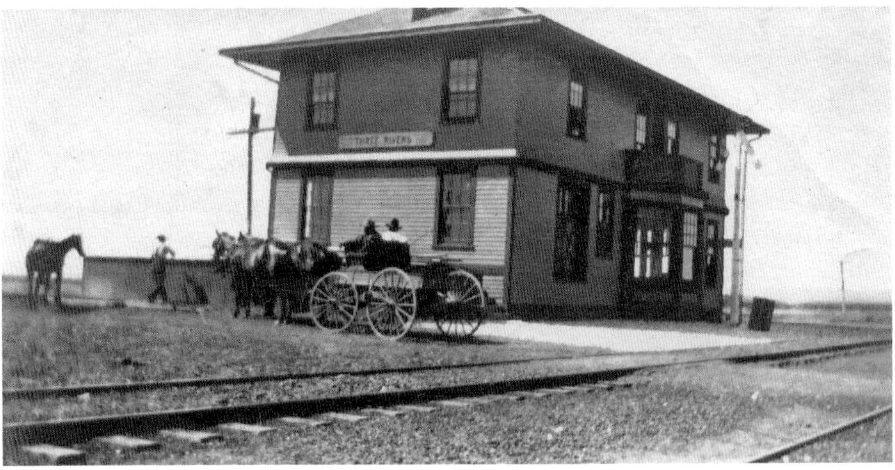

Three Rivers railroad depot, circa 1940. *Photograph courtesy of Tularosa Basin Historical Society, Image P349.*

Children from the valley, including Mescaleros from the Shanta families, attended school at Three Rivers. The school closed in 1948, when buses began taking the children to school in Tularosa.

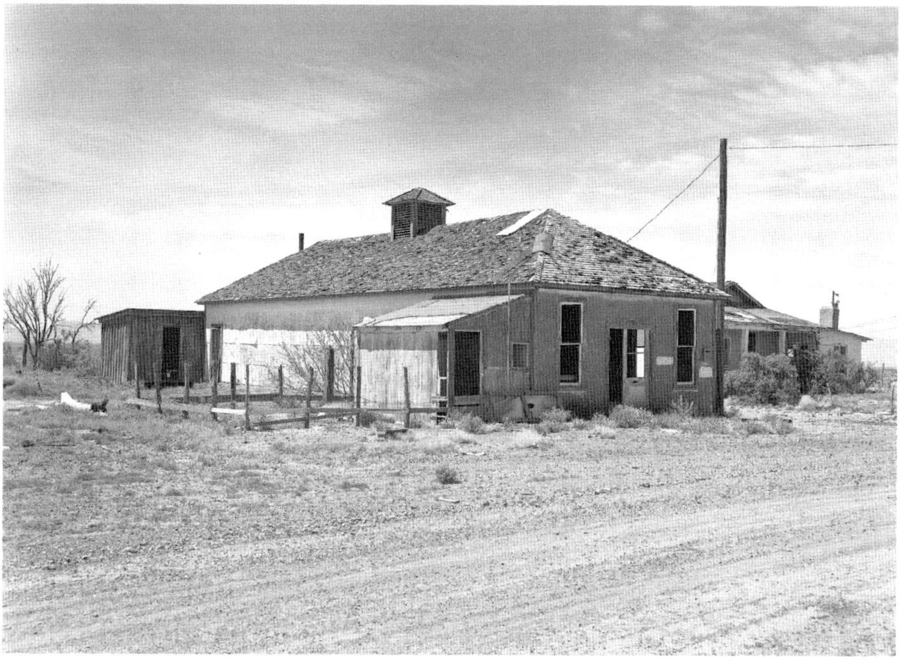

Old general store and post office near railroad tracks, 1958. *Photo courtesy of New Mexico State University Library, Archives and Special Collections, Image 02860107.*

Houses for the railroad workers lined both sides of the track until the late 1940s, when the railroad no longer needed water for its steam engines due to a switch to electric engines, and there was no longer a need for a railroad siding.

The focal point of present-day Three Rivers is the Three Rivers Trading Post, which at various times housed a saloon, bar, restaurant and post office. Mail went out by train twice a day. Alonzo Love put in the bar, and customers could order some food. Noted New Mexico author Tony Hillerman stated that the crew from the White Sands Missile Range used to have coffee there in the morning, and he figured out it was time to shoot a missile when they all left. G.L. Tucker commented:

> *I worked at the Three Rivers store when I was in high school. I hauled off the trash. Shorty Miller owned the store. Shorty had two wooden legs where a train had run over his leg. As time permitted, I would do heavier work for him. As he got older, he couldn't stay on his legs and decided he was going to sell the store.* [He] *was negotiating the sale of the store, and I was stocking shelves. He came in and said we have a deal but he wouldn't sell unless the*

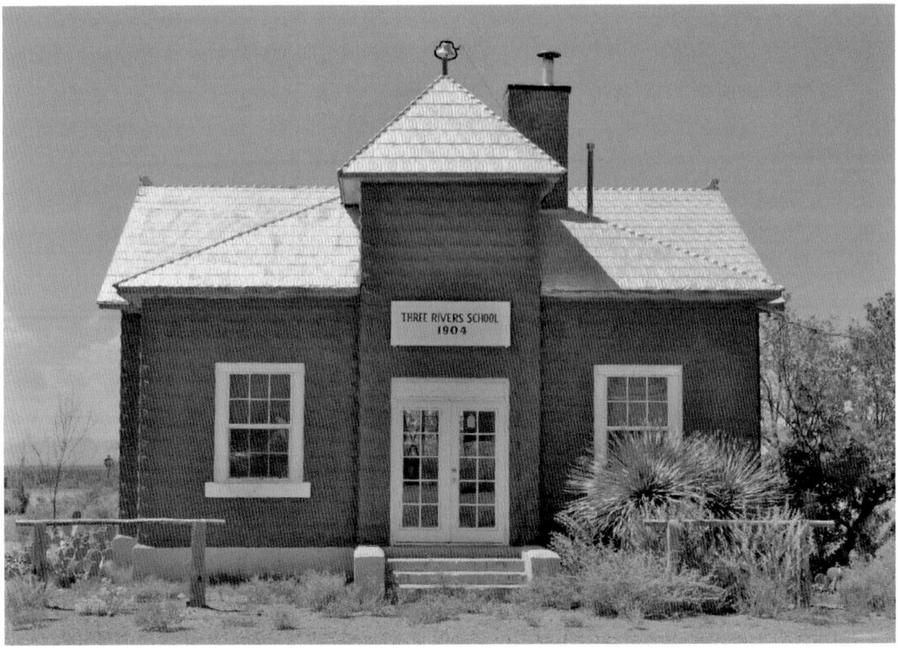

Three Rivers School, built in 1904. *Photo courtesy of Doyle Cozzens.*

> *new owners gave me a job. We tried to figure out what he was paying me as he just gave me money when I went to town as salary. Deal he agreed to with the new owners was for $2.50 an hour.*
>
> *Bar/café, general store, back was PO, the front filling station. Alonzo Love bought the store from Shorty Miller. If you can sell gas, I will set you up to fix flats. Semi drove up, and I filled gas for $0.25 a gallon. Kenneth Nosker bought the store next. At that time, Kenneth also had the Woodside place and then him and his partners bought the Stover Ranch.*[194]

The building also housed a telegraph station for a time while that was the means of communications. The main operator was a man named Frank Woodside.

Rumor has it that a U.S. postal inspector came into the trading post about 1975. At that time, the postmaster, Cheney Morrow, was also the storekeeper and barkeep. The postal inspector sat in the trading post unannounced just watching the activities. After a time of observing what was occurring, he had Morrow arrested, and on that day, Three Rivers lost its post office and zip code. Morrow was later convicted and sent to federal prison at La Tuna.

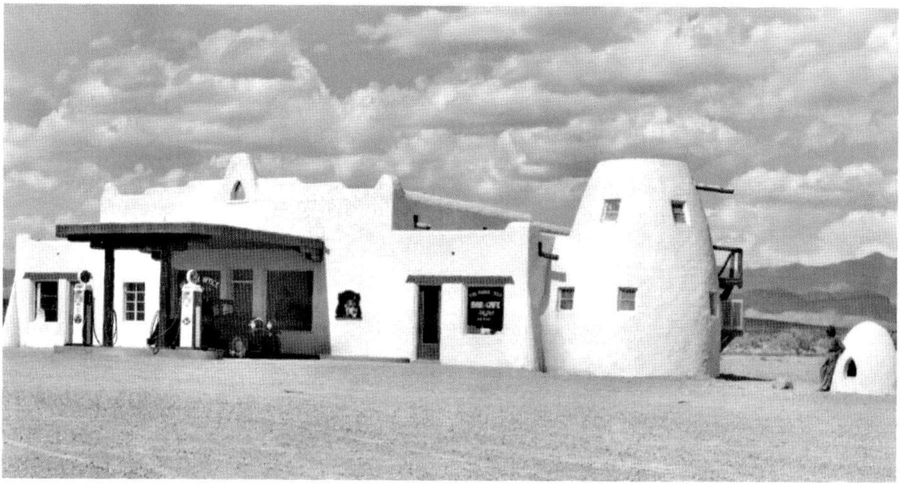

Three Rivers General Store, circa 1950. *Photo courtesy of Richard Bryant.*

In 1972, a portion of the ranch was sold to C.H. Leavell of El Paso, Texas. Leavell hired Harold Shepperd as ranch foreman and set aside forty acres for Human Systems Research, Inc., to conduct archaeological surveys of the region.

In 1977, the ranch was sold to Sonny Wright from the Fort Sumner/Roswell area, who paid $2 million for fifty-four thousand acres. Wright, a professional rodeo cowboy, won the world steer roping title in 1965.

Hired to manage the game on the ranch was Wright's friend Bobby Maes. Tommy Skipworth was hired as horse trainer for twenty-five horses. Harold Shepperd, who had worked for Ryan and then Leavell, was hired by Wright as ranch manager. Included in the purchase of the ranch was a herd of one thousand white-faced Hereford cattle. Although the ranch was abundant in wild game, Wright did not allow hunting for two years in order to increase his herd. Wright owned the ranch for seven years before selling it to Roswell oilman Colin McMillan.

McMillan, born in Houston, graduated from the University of North Carolina with a degree in geology. He served as an engineer officer on active duty in the United States Marine Corps from 1957 until 1960 and then in the marine corps reserve until 1972, when he was discharged with the rank of major.

Moving to Roswell, New Mexico, in 1961, McMillan served in the New Mexico State Legislature from 1971 to 1982 and as minority whip for four years. He ran for lieutenant governor in 1982 and for governor in 1986, losing in both attempts. In 1994, he ran for the U.S. Senate but was defeated by incumbent Jeff Bingaman.

During the George H.W. Bush presidency in 1990–92, McMillan was assistant secretary of defense for installations and logistics. He was New Mexico state chairman of George W. Bush's 2000 presidential campaign and then president of the Sallie Mae student loan program from 2001 to 2003.

In addition, McMillan was chairman and CEO of the Permian Exploration Company, chairman of the First Federal Savings Bank (Roswell, New Mexico) and the founder and CEO of McMillan Production Company.[195]

When Colin McMillan bought the Three Rivers Ranch in 1984, he immediately recognized the need for water. To that end, he installed twenty miles of pipeline to water the ranch in areas not watered in the past, thus allowing the land to recover after being overgrazed by his four hundred head of cattle. Eventually, McMillan's efforts allowed over 90 percent of his fifty-four thousand acres to be within one-mile walking distance for his cattle. McMillan also discovered that windmills were expensive to maintain and abandoned them in favor of a gravity-fed pipeline system.

The bottomland area of the ranch continued as farmland growing alfalfa as a cash crop and winter wheat to feed the ranch livestock. Hydrostatic pressure moved the water to a moveable sprinkler system with all crops rotated in different pastures. Pastures were burned every three years to control mesquite, greasewood and other nonedible plants.[196]

McMillan next tapped the cool, pure mountain spring water to form the Sierra Water Company. He established a twenty-foot well near one of the springs and ran the water to a loading facility one thousand feet away, where it was loaded in trucks and shipped to Portales for bottling.

To oversee these operations, McMillan employed Glen Anderson as ranch foreman/manager, Randell Joyce as ranch business manager and Sam Reagan as cattle manager.

Glen and Peggy Anderson moved into the old Fall Library House in about 1982 to manage the property for the next eleven years. Anderson had previously managed the Harvey Yates farm north of Tularosa. Anderson retired in 2001, and Sam Reagan and his wife, Julia, assumed duties as ranch managers.

The Three Rivers Ranch was a working ranch, and cowboys were injured from time to time. A particularly devastating injury occurred when Sam Reagan's son was paralyzed in an automobile accident shortly after high school.

Unfortunately, on July 23, 2003, McMillan took his own life at the ranch. He was sixty-seven years old and awaiting confirmation as secretary of the navy under President George W. Bush. McMillan was survived by his wife, Kay; four children; and eight grandchildren.[197]

9

A Final Accounting

The McMillan family still owns the Three Rivers Ranch, with Sam Reagan continuing as ranch manager as of this writing. The Bureau of Land Management manages the petroglyphs from its Las Cruces field office, and the U.S. Forest Service manages a campground at the western edge of Sierra Blanca. The Shanta community of the Mescalero Apache Reservation still exists, as does the San Patricio Catholic Church. And descendants of the burros purchased in the 1950s still roam the ranch and the western environs of Sierra Blanca.

On any given day, a person seeking a spot for quiet reflection can climb the ridge lined by the petroglyphs overlooking the Three Rivers Valley and imagine the Jornada Mogollon chipping images into the rocks. Looking to the east would be Shanta Boy and his family driving their five thousand head of sheep or Father Braun building the San Patricio Chapel. Perhaps standing in the Shanta community would be Virginia Shanta Klinecole and Sarah Misquez.

Susan McSween Barber might appear with her hands on her hips staring out into the distance. Perhaps Billy the Kid might be visible talking to Patrick Coghlan in his latest effort to sell Coghlan stolen cattle. Pete Crawford drives his cattle to the north of Santo Nino chapel. Small farmers and ranch hands from over the generations might be tending and irrigating their crops. Turning to the west, the wagon carrying the Nesmiths and their daughter heads toward the White Sands. Tom Ryan can be seen climbing out of his airplane at the airstrip behind his house. Or Colin McMillan could be gazing toward Sierra Blanca, contemplating the geology of the valley.

At the old library wing of Albert Bacon Fall's house, the former senator might be conferring with Oliver Lee and developing a strategy for his defense in the murder of Albert Fountain, or with Wayne Brazel contemplating his defense in a trial for the murder of Pat Garrett. The companion of Fall might be Edward Doheny, discussing the oil reserves at Elk Hill or Teapot Dome. Jack Fall could be talking to his father about their plans for the Three Rivers Ranch. Then again, Fall might have his arm around his grandson Albert Fall Chase before the young man goes to the Philippine Islands shortly before the start of World War II, never to be seen again.

The personalities and the names have changed over the years, but not the valley's mystique. What is certain is this: Three Rivers has occupied a special place in the world since the first Jornada Mogollon gazed on the fertile valley. Every person who has seen the valley since then has stood in awe of its natural beauty and grandeur. It still happens today.

Notes

Introduction

1. Wimberly, Rogers and Eidenbach, "Archeology Survey," 27.
2. Volumes have been written about the Teapot Dome Scandal and its effect on Albert Bacon Fall. I have tried to limit its relationship to Three Rivers in this book. For more information, see, among others, Weisner, *Politics of Justice*, and Stratton, *Tempest Over Teapot Dome*. Additionally, Stratton points out that there are three main repositories for Fall papers: Huntington Library, San Marino, California, with fifty-four linear feet for the years 1887–1941; University of New Mexico Library, Albuquerque, New Mexico, with nine linear feet for the years 1916–27; and the New Mexico State University State University Library in Las Cruces with two and a half linear feet covering the years 1907–41, (Stratton, page 350). Stratton is also the editor of Fall's memoirs, which cover the senator's early life to 1891.

Chapter 1

3. Bussey, Kelly and Southward, *LA 4921*, 120–21.
4. Lehmer, "Jornada Branch."
5. Bussey, Kelly and Southward, *LA 4921*, 127.
6. Ibid., 127–29.
7. Sanders, *Oldest Book*, 11–14.

8. Wimberly, Rogers and Eidenbach, "Archeological Survey."
9. Duran and Crotty, *Three Rivers Petroglyph Site*, 21.
10. Cosgrove and Cosgrove, *Cosgrove Report.*
11. Ibid., 1.
12. Ibid., 5.
13. Wimberly, Rogers and Edinbach, "Archaeological Survey," 255.
14. Bussey, Kelly and Southward, *LA 4921*, 129–30.
15. Duran and Crotty, *Three Rivers Petroglyph Site*, 19.
16. Schaafsma, *Rock Art*, 71–72.
17. Ibid., 63–64.
18. Ibid., 74–77. This is perhaps the best synopsis of interpretation of the petroglyphs.
19. McClusky, "Hatchet Site."
20. Wimberly, Rogers and Edinbach, "Archaeological Survey," 143–45.
21. Mera and Stallings, *Lincoln Black on Red.*

CHAPTER 2

22. Duran and Crotty, *Three Rivers Petroglyph Site*, 15.
23. Opler and Opler, "Mescalero Apache History in the Southwest," 38.
24. Sonnichsen, *Mescalero Apaches*, 106–13.
25. Marilyn Cozzens comments to Gary Cozzens, August 16, 2014.
26. Ball, *Indeh*, 233.
27. Tiswin was made by growing corn in large containers until it sprouted and was then crushed. The corn fermented, and the resulting beverage was like beer, only stronger and more potent.
28. Ball, *Indeh*, 296.
29. Ibid., 297–99.
30. Simms, ed., *Cowboys, Indians and Pulpits*, 28.
31. Ibid., 30–31.
32. Ball, *Indeh*, 299.
33. Ibid.
34. Cave, *God's Warrior*, 364.
35. Ibid., 79–80.
36. Ball, *Indeh*, 233.
37. Cave, *God's Warrior*, 193.
38. Ball, *Indeh*, 234; Emerson, *Among the Mescalero Apaches*, 137.
39. G.L. Tucker interview with Gary Cozzens on September 27, 2014.

CHAPTER 3

40. Santiago, "Into Lands Totally Unknown," 1–26.
41. Neal, *Captive Mountain Water*, 68.
42. Wimberly, Rogers and Edinbach, "Archeology Survey," 455.
43. Ibid., 458.
44. Ibid., 460–61.
45. Heitzler, *Meanwhile, Back at the Ranch*, 102.
46. Marilyn Cozzens comments to Gary Cozzens, August 19, 2014.
47. Keleher, *Fabulous Frontier*, 115.
48. Furman, "In the Mountain's Shadow," 4.
49. Ibid., 8.
50. Ibid., 4.
51. Wilson, ed., *Pat Garrett*, 84.
52. Ibid., 45.
53. Ibid., 68.
54. Ibid., 69–71.
55. Ibid., 45 and 163, n3. Although John Meadows says at one point that Nesmith was Coghlan's foreman and again that he was manager of Pat Coghlan's Three Rivers farm at the time of his death (August 17, 1882), Meadows also says that after court adjourned in the spring, Coghlan had no more use for either Meadows or the Nesmiths. From the information available, it appears more likely that Coghlan had ceased to employ Nesmith, who was working as Meadows's partner at the latter's Three Rivers ranch or farm at the time of the Nesmith murders.
56. *Tularosa Valley Tribune*, January 28, 1911.
57. Sawey, *Charles A. Siringo*, 67.
58. Ibid., 67.
59. Ibid., 71–72.
60. Furman, "In the Mountain's Shadow," 10.
61. Sawey, *Charles A. Siringo*, 72.
62. Ibid., 73.
63. *Santa Fe New Mexican*, April 22, 1882.
64. Ibid.
65. One would presume that William H. Bonney, aka Billy the Kid, would have also been called to testify, but he had been killed on July 14, 1881, at Fort Sumner by Pat Garrett. It is interesting to speculate what he might have said about Coghlan's rustling activities.
66. Sonnichsen, *Tularosa*, 252–56.
67. Furman, "In the Mountain's Shadow," 11.

68. Rasch, "Nesmith Murder Mystery," 16.
69. *Rio Grande Republican*, September 9, 1882.
70. Ibid., September 16, 1882.
71. Ibid., September 23, 1882.
72. Furman, "In the Mountain's Shadow," 12.
73. Rasch, "Nesmith Murder Mystery," 18.
74. *Rio Grande Republican*, March 21, 1885.
75. Ibid., April 4, 1885; Wilson, ed., *Pat Garrett*, 93–94.
76. *Rio Grande Republican*, May 2, 1885.
77. L'Aloge, *Ghosts and Mysteries*.
78. *Santa Fe New Mexican*, November 4, 1885.
79. *Rio Grande Republican*, April 29, 1882.
80. Furman, "In the Mountain's Shadow," 14.
81. Sonnichsen, *Tularosa*, 257.
82. Furman, "In the Mountain's Shadow," 15.
83. Miller, "Women of Lincoln County," 189.
84. Nolan, *Lincoln County War*, 436.
85. Haldane, "Susan McSween's Diamonds," 39.v
86. Ibid.; Furman, "In the Mountain's Shadow," 17–18.
87. Simms, ed., *Cowboys, Indians and Pulpits*, 24–26.
88. Keleher, *Fabulous Frontier*, 244.
89. Duran and Crotty, *Three Rivers Petroglyph Site*, 17.
90. Simms, ed., *Cowboys, Indians and Pulpits*, 26.
91. Ibid., 4–6.
92. Ibid., 20.
93. Ibid., 22.
94. Ibid., 22–26.
95. Ibid., 32–33.
96. Ibid., 40–41.
97. Ibid., 41–43.
98. Ibid., 43.
99. Ibid., 45.
100. Ibid., 46.
101. Ibid., 26.
102. Furman, "In the Mountain's Shadow," 3–4.
103. Keleher, *Fabulous Frontier*, 219–20, footnote 4.

Chapter 4

104. Stratton, ed., *Memoirs of Albert B. Fall*, provides a biography of Fall's early years.
105. Furman, "In the Mountain's Shadow," 20.
106. Sonnichsen, *Tularosa*, 257.
107. Owen, *Two Alberts*, 423.
108. Sonnichsen, *Tularosa*, 263.
109. Welsh, *Dunes and Dreams*, 19–25.
110. Ball, *Indeh*, 283.
111. Keleher, *Fabulous Frontier*, 190.
112. Furman, "In the Mountain's Shadow," 22.
113. Neal, *Captive Mountain Waters*, 66.
114. Ibid.
115. Sonnichsen, *Tularosa*, 270–71.
116. Stratton, *Tempest Over Teapot Dome*, 152.
117. Owen, *Two Alberts*, 398.
118. Furman, "In the Mountain's Shadow," 30–33.
119. Sonnichsen, *Tularosa*, 265.
120. Dahl, "Albert Bacon Fall," 10.
121. Weisner, *Politics of Justice*, 6.
122. Ibid., 10–11.
123. Ibid., 10–11.
124. Nelson, "Do Not Offend," 35–36.
125. Dahl, "Albert Bacon Fall," 10–11.
126. Nelson, "Do Not Offend," 37.
127. Ibid., 38.
128. Furman, "In the Mountain's Shadow," 27–28.
129. Keleher, *Fabulous Frontier*, 230.
130. Cave, *God's Warrior*, 196.
131. Nelson, "Do Not Offend," 37.
132. Weisner, *Politics of Justice*, 208–09.
133. Stratton, *Tempest Over Teapot Dome*, 236.
134. Stratton, ed., *Memoirs of Albert B. Fall*, 54. Just before going to prison, Fall was diagnosed with severe hardening of the arteries, a chronic heart ailment, disabling arthritis, chronic but inactive tuberculosis and pleurisy.
135. Keleher, *Fabulous Frontier*, 228.
136. Stratton, *Tempest Over Teapot Dome*, 237.
137. Weisner, *Politics of Justice*, 210.
138. Ibid.

139. Ibid., 211.
140. Ibid., 208.
141. Ibid.
142. Stratton, *Tempest Over Teapot Dome*, 339.
143. Ibid.
144. *El Paso Times*, August 16, 1935, 8.
145. Ibid., August 15, 1935, 2.
146. Cave, *God's Warrior*, 195.
147. Keleher, *Fabulous Frontier*, 200.
148. Emerson, *Among the Mescalero Apaches*, 155.
149. Ibid.
150. Shockley, "Life and Death," 11–33.
151. *El Paso Herald-Post*, March 25, 1943, 1.
152. Keleher, *Fabulous Frontier*, 209.
153. Curry, *George Curry*, 300–01.
154. Keleher, *Fabulous Frontier*, 209–10.
155. Weisner, *Politics of Justice*.

Chapter 5

156. Tucker, interview, September 27, 2014.
157. Spencer, interview, September 21, 2014.
158. Tucker, interview, September 27, 2014.

Chapter 6

159. Neal, *Captive Mountain Waters*, 74.
160. Ryan, interview, September 8, 2014.
161. Ibid.
162. Ibid., August 28, 2014. A man and woman whose name was Shanta showed up at Tom Ryan IV's funeral and told Victoria that Tom was their father. When asked by Victoria, Amador Martinez, the former ranch foreman, said he thought the claim was true.
163. Sonnichsen, *Tularosa*, 270–72.
164. Heitzler, *Meanwhile, Back at the Ranch*, 147.
165. Cozzens, interview, August 16, 2104.
166. Heitzler, *Meanwhile, Back at the Ranch*, 147.

167. Cozzens, interview, August 16, 2014.
168. Furman, "In the Mountain's Shadow," 60–61.
169. Heitzler, *Meanwhile, Back at the Ranch*, 12–22.
170. Cave, *God's Warrior*, 460–61.
171. Furman, "In the Mountain's Shadow," 62.
172. Tucker, interview, September 27, 2014.
173. Cozzens, interview, August 16, 2014.
174. Furman, "In the Mountain's Shadow," 62; Ryan, interview, September 12, 2014.
175. Heitzler, *Meanwhile, Back at the Ranch*, 36.
176. Cozzens, interview, August 16, 2014.
177. Sonnichsen, *Tularosa*, 272.
178. Furman, "Lulu to Lassos," 50–57.

Chapter 7

179. Neal, *Captive Mountain Waters*, 67.
180. At this time, the railroads used steam engines, and the water in the Tularosa Basin was corrosive and ruined the steam engines. As a result, mountain water was piped down from the Sacramento Mountains to points in the basin.
181. Neal, *Captive Mountain Waters*, 67.
182. Ibid., 68.
183. Ibid.
184. Ibid., 68–69.
185. Ibid., 69–70.
186. Ibid., 70.
187. Ibid., 70–71.
188. Ibid.
189. Ibid., 72. Mrs. Fall conducted all of the ranch operations while her husband was incarcerated in prison after being convicted in the Teapot Dome affair.
190. Ibid., 72–73.
191. Ibid., 73.
192. Tucker, interview, September 27, 2014.

Chapter 8

193. Ibid.
194. Ibid.
195. *Los Angeles Times*, "Colin McMillan, 67; Oilman, Navy Secretary Nominee," July 25, 2003, http://articles.latimes.com/2003/jul/25/local/me-mcmillan25 (accessed August 18, 2014).
196. Furman, "In the Mountain's Shadow," 68.
197. *Los Angeles Times*, "Colin McMillan"; Furman, "In the Mountain's Shadow," 70.

Bibliography

Ball, Eve. *Indeh: An Apache Odyssey*. With Nora Henn and Lynda Sanchez. Norman: University of Oklahoma Press, 1988.

Beckett, Patrick H., and Regge N. Wisemann. *Jornada Mogollon Archaeology: Proceedings of the First Jornada Conference*. Las Cruces: New Mexico State University, 1979.

Bethune, Martha Fall. *Race with the Wind: The Personal Life of Albert B. Fall*. El Paso, TX: Novio Books, 1989.

Bussey, Stanley D., Richard Kelly and Judith Southward. *LA 4921, Three Rivers, Otero County, New Mexico: A Project of Excavation, Stabilization, and Interpretation of a Prehistoric Village*. Las Cruces, NM: Bureau of Land Management, 1976.

Cave, Dorothy. *God's Warrior: Father Albert Braun, OFM 1889–1983, Last of the Frontier Priests*. Santa Fe, NM: Sunstone Press, 2011.

Cosgrove, H.S., and C.B. Cosgrove. *The Cosgrove Report: A Preliminary Survey of the El Paso Pueblo District*. El Paso, TX: El Paso Archeological Society, Special Report #3, 1965.

Curry, George. *George Curry: 1861–1947, An Autobiography*. Albuquerque: University of New Mexico Press, 1958.

Dahl, Patrick. "Albert Bacon Fall: New Mexico's Connection with a 1920s Scandal," *Enchantment Magazine*, June 1987.

Dike, Shelton H. *The Territorial Post Offices of New Mexico*. Albuquerque, NM: Privately published by Dr. S.H. Dike, 1958.

Duran, Meliha, and Helen K. Crotty. *Three Rivers Petroglyph Site: Results of the ASNM Rock Art Recording Field School*. Albuquerque: Archaeological Society of New Mexico, 1999.

Emerson, Dorothy. *Among the Mescalero Apaches: The Story of Father Albert Braun, OFM*. Tucson: University of Arizona Press, 1973.

Furman, Janie Bell. "In the Mountain's Shadow: Three Rivers Ranch." *Pioneer* (Tularosa Basin Historical Society) 9, nos. 1–2 (2005).

———. "Lulu to Lassos: The Bill Trammell Story." *Pioneer* (Tularosa Basin Historical Society) 17, no. 1 (2012).

———. "Pat Coghlan, King of Tularosa." *2009 Tularosa Basin Conference Proceedings*, Edited by David H. Greenwald, Basin Exploration, Settlement, Entrepreneurs and Development.

Haldane, Roberta K. "What Became of Susan McSween's Diamonds?" *Southern New Mexico Historical Review* (Dona Ana County Historical Society) 6, no. 1 (January 1999).

Heitzler, Gretchen. *Meanwhile, Back at the Ranch*. Albuquerque, NM: Hidden Valley Press, 1980.

Jensen, Joan M., and Darlis A. Miller. *New Mexico Women: Intercultural Perspectives*. Albuquerque: University of New Mexico Press, 1986.

Julyan, Robert. *The Mountains of New Mexico*. Albuquerque: University of New Mexico Press, 2006.

———. *The Place Names of New Mexico*. Albuquerque: University of New Mexico Press, 1996.

Keleher, William. *The Fabulous Frontier*. Albuquerque: University of New Mexico Press, 1945.

———. *Violence in Lincoln County*. Albuquerque: University of New Mexico Press, 1957.

L'Aloge, Bob. *Ghosts and Mysteries of the Old West*. Las Cruces, NM: Yucca Tree Press, 1990.

Lehmer, Donald J. "The Jornada Branch of the Mogollon." *University of Arizona Social Science Bulletin* 17 (1948).

McClusky, Eugene B. "The Hatchet Site: A Preliminary Report." *Southwestern Lore* 26, no. 4 (1961).

Mera, H.P., and W.S. Stallings Jr. *Lincoln Black on Red: Laboratory of Anthropology, Archaeological Survey, Technical Series, Bulletin No. 2*. October 10, 1931.

Metz, Leon C. *Pat Garrett: The Story of a Western Lawman*. Norman: University of Oklahoma Press, 1974.

Miller, Darlis A. *The California Column in New Mexico*. Albuquerque: University of New Mexico Press, 1982.

———. "The Women of Lincoln County, 1860–1900." In *New Mexico Women Intercultural Perspectives*, edited by Joan M. Jenson and Darlis A. Miller. Albuquerque: University of New Mexico Press, 1986.

Neal, Dorothy Jensen. *Captive Mountain Waters: A Unique Chapter in the History of Southern New Mexico*. El Paso: Texas Western Press, 1961.

Nelson, Morgan. "Do Not Offend the Priests of Amun: An Analysis of the Teapot Dome Scandal and Albert B. Fall." *Journal of Wild West History* 4, no. 6 (December, 2011).

Nolan, Frederick. E-mail correspondence with the author, February 14, 2012.

———. *The Lincoln County War: A Documentary History*. Norman: University of Oklahoma Press, 1992.

Oates, Yvonne R., and Glenn S. Russell. *Archaeology of the Mogollon Highlands: Settlement Systems and Adaptations, Volume 1. Defining the Mogollon*. Santa Fe: Museum of New Mexico Office of Archeological Studies, Laboratory of Anthropology Notes 232, 1999.

Opler, Morris Edward, and Barbara H. Opler. "Mescalero Apache History in the Southwest." *New Mexico Historical Review* 21, no. 1 (January 1950).

Owen, Gordon R. *The Two Alberts: Fountain and Fall*. Las Cruces, NM: Yucca Tree Press, 1996.

Rasch, Phillip. "The Nesmith Murder Mystery." *Denver Westerners Monthly Roundup* 17, no. 5 (May 1961): 16–20.

Reily-Branum, Barbara Jeanne, and Roberta Key Haldane. *Corralled in Old Lincoln County, New Mexico: The Lin Branum Family of Coyote Canyon and the I Bar X*. Alamogordo, NM: Bennett Printing, Inc., 1995.

Sanders, Joe Ben. *Give Me That Old Time Religion: Migration of the Ancestral Hopi from the Three Rivers Area to the Socorro Area En Route to the Hopi Mesas*. Bent, NM: Center of the Universe Press, 2001 (revised 2002).

———. *The History of Bent, New Mexico*. Bent, NM: Center of the Universe Press, 2001.

———. *The Oldest Book in America: Three Rivers Petroglyph Site, Rock Writings of the Ancestral Hopi*. Bent, NM: Center of the Universe Press, 2000 (revised 2002).

———. *Reading Jornada Mogollon Rock Writings or Why I Never Saw a White Man Read a Petroglyph*. Bent, NM: Center of the Universe Press, 2003.

———. *The Rock Archaeologist: Clan Migrations of the Jornada Mogollon Hopi and Casas Grande Hopi En Route to the Hopi Mesa*. Bent, NM: Mogollon Hopi Archaeological Society, 2003.

———. *Three Rivers Petroglyph Site: A Self-Guided Tour Book*. Bent, NM: Center of the Universe Press, 2003.

Santiago, Mark. "Into Lands Totally Unknown, Spanish Expeditions into the Sacramento Mountains." *2009 Tularosa Basin Conference Proceedings*. Edited by David H. Greenwald, Basin Exploration, Settlement, Entrepreneurs and Development.

Sawey, Orlan. *Charles A. Siringo*. Boston: Twayne Publishers, 1981.

Schaafsma, Polly. *Rock Art in New Mexico*. Albuquerque: University of New Mexico Press, 1992.

Shockley, Nancy E. "The Life and Death of First Lieutenant Albert Fall Chase." *Southern New Mexico Historical Review* 6 (2004).

Simms, D. Harper, ed. *Cowboys, Indians and Pulpits: The Memoirs of J. Denton Simms*. Albuquerque, NM: Los Hemanos Publications, 1982.

Sonnichsen, C.L. *The Mescalero Apaches*. Norman: University of Oklahoma Press, 1958.

———. *Tularosa: Last of the Frontier West*. Albuquerque: University of New Mexico Press, 1960.

Spoerl, Patricia M. *A Brief History of the Early Years of the Lincoln National Forest*. Lincoln, NM: Lincoln National Forest, February 1981.

———. *Thousands of Years of Use: Prehistory and History of the Lincoln National Forest*. Lincoln, NM: Lincoln National Forest, December 1983.

Stratton, David H., ed. *The Memoirs of Albert B. Fall*. El Paso, TX: University of El Paso Press, 1966.

———. *Tempest Over Teapot Dome*. Norman: University of Oklahoma Press, 1998.

Stuart, D.E., and R.P. Gauthier. *Prehistoric New Mexico: Background for Survey*. Santa Fe, NM: Historic Preservation Bureau, 1981.

Sutherlin, Kay. "Petroglyphs at Three Rivers, New Mexico." *The Artifact* (El Paso Archaeological Society) 16, no. 2, (1978).

Weisner, Herman B. *The Politics of Justice: A.B. Fall and the Teapot Dome Scandal*. Albuquerque, NM: Creative Designs, 1988.

Welsh, Michael. *Dunes and Dreams: A History of White Sands National Monument*. Santa Fe, NM: Intermountain Cultural Resource Center, 1995.

Wilson, John P., ed. *Pat Garrett and Billy the Kid as I Knew Them: Reminiscences of John P. Meadows*. Albuquerque: University of New Mexico Press, 2004.

Wimberly, Mark, Alan Rogers and Peter Eidenbach. "Archeology Survey, Three Rivers Drainage, New Mexico." *The Artifact* (El Paso Archaeological Society) 15 (1977).

NEWSPAPERS

Alamogordo (NM) Daily News
El Paso (TX) Herald-Post
El Paso (TX) Times
Los Angeles Times
Rio Grande Republican (Las Cruces, NM)
Santa Fe New Mexican
Tularosa (NM) Valley Tribune

INTERVIEWS

Marilyn Cozzens
Victoria Ryan
Steven Spencer
G.L. Tucker

Index

About the Author

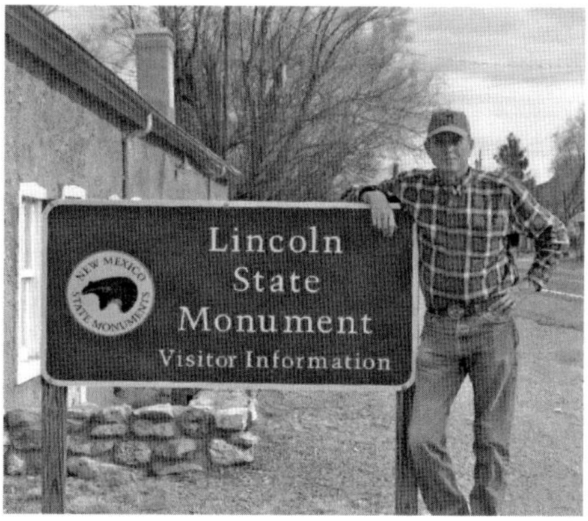

A native New Mexican, Gary Cozzens grew up in Portales, where he graduated from Eastern New Mexico University, earning a double major in history and political science. Following graduation, he served in the United States Marine Corps for a total of twenty-four years, including Operation Desert Storm, and retired as a major in 1999. Cozzens is currently the manager of the Lincoln Historic Site in Lincoln. He is a member of the Lincoln County Historical Society, the Museum of New Mexico Foundation, the Historical Society of New Mexico and the Friends of Historic Lincoln. He is the author of *The Nogal Mesa* and *Capitan, New Mexico*, also published by The History Press. Gary and his wife, Shirley Crawford, live on the Nogal Mesa in Lincoln County, New Mexico.

Visit us at
www.historypress.net

This title is also available as an e-book